FOUR STEPS TO A BETTER LIFE

THE BIG FOUR PROCESS

DR. ANTHONY DECANTO

CONTENTS

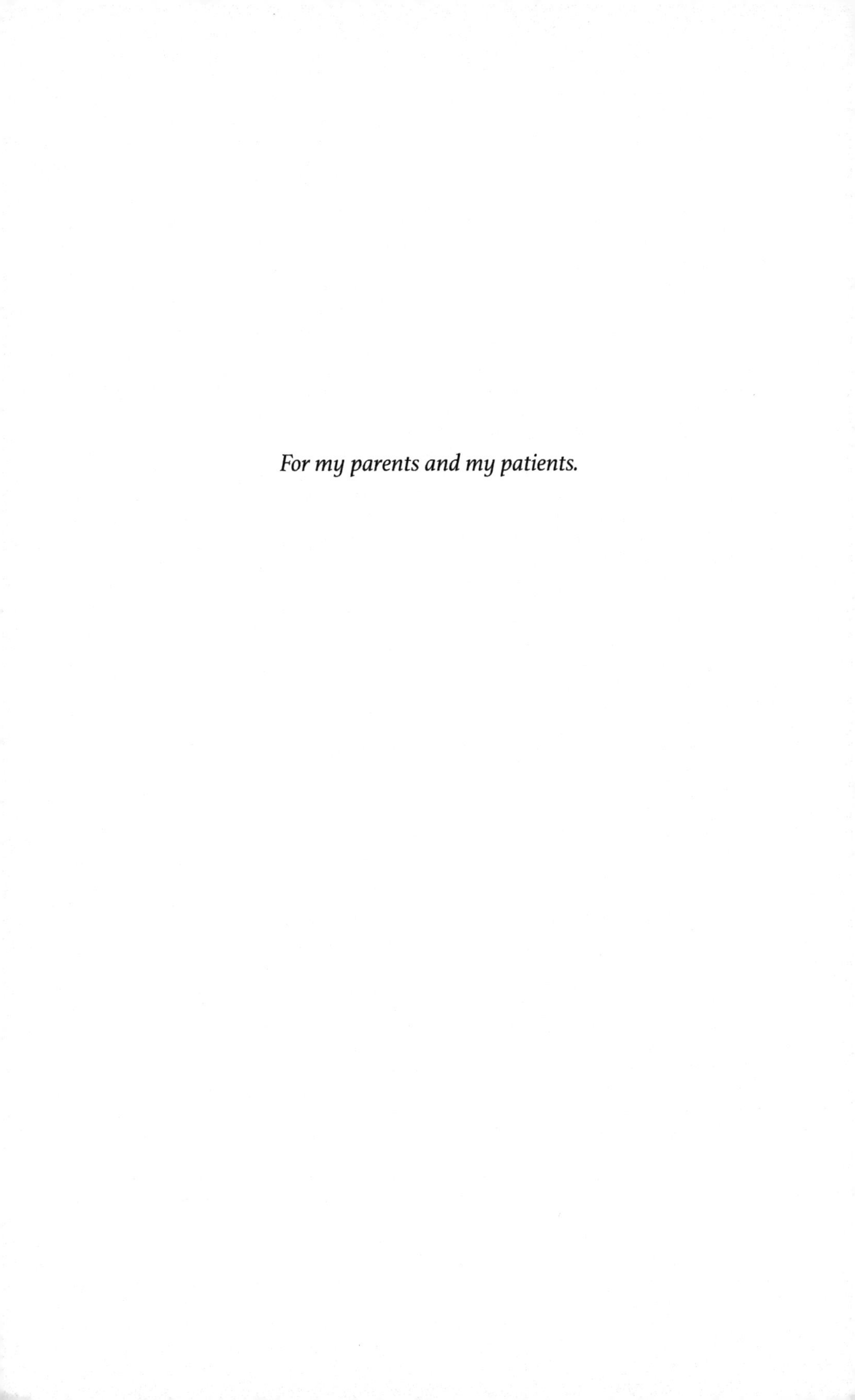

For my parents and my patients.

FOREWORD

The only constant in the universe is change. This applies to all aspects of our existence from the day of our birth to our death. Some changes are a benefit to society, while others are a detriment. A major situation faced in society today is not only disease-- chronic, acute, and terminal, i.e., cancer, diabetes, arthritis, heart disease, auto-immune disease, depression, obesity, dementia, and other physical illnesses-- but also dysfunctional personal situations that can be just as dangerous and deadly.

Although the government, medical research centers, and the pharmaceutical companies spend billions of dollars each year to alleviate diseases, cures either do not work or do not bring all patients back to optimal health. There is something missing from the present model of health care since health care is failing so many patients. With all the efforts of improving our medical model by new research, new pharmaceuticals, and new protocols, society is still losing the battle.

Science and medicine only follow the lifecycle of a disease, which is easier to follow than someone's personal circumstance.

It is easy to trace the cycle of a bacterium through the physical aspect of our anatomy, then understanding its interaction with the energetic aspect of the human body.

That is what the medical model is missing, the energetic aspect. Science and medicine create new drugs and new therapies to correct dysfunctions of the body. Yet, there is a lack of scientific knowledge in medical research, for understanding the interactive life cycle of the state of well-being with the state of sickness. In *Four Steps to A Better Life,* you will learn about a new connection, not only to your physical health, but also to the other situations in your life, such as controlling your weight, getting in shape, improving family and work situations, dealing with problems in your relationships, and more.

After reading *Four Steps to A Better Life,* you will see and understand the subtle connections of the physical body and how your energetic thoughts create a mental image, which produces an emotion, that then can alter matter, resulting in either a positive or negative conclusion depending on your thoughts.

INTRODUCTION

Hello and welcome. I am so glad you have chosen to spend some time with me today. I am Dr. Tony, and I am going to help you learn about a new healing art that I have developed. It is not part of the conventional healing arts today, but I am confident that as people learn of what I have created, more will use it to help them break through entrenched, unproductive behavior patterns and create the life they desire.

I am a no-nonsense meat and potatoes type of person, so I am going to get to the point quickly. After all, your time is just as valuable as mine! This new healing modality is the culmination of my life's work and has taken me over 40 years to develop. In my eyes, this was not created by accident, but by divine inspiration. I hope you are as excited to learn about it as I am to explain it!

In 1979, I started my chiropractic practice. I saw both remarkable positive changes in some patients, as well as no changes in other patients. This piqued my scientific curiosity. I began searching for a deeper understanding of why some people were able to see results and others were not. Deep in my soul, I knew something was missing in my chiropractic practice, but I couldn't quite pinpoint what that was. It was a vague, ever-present feeling.

I knew it was somehow related to God and spirit, and their connection with every individual walking on this earth. I had the realization one day when a patient came to see me that what informs a person's ability to heal and get better is what I now call their personal narrative. We will delve deeper into the meaning of this idea as we proceed through this learning experience, but for the moment, let's define a personal narrative as a person's experience throughout their life and how that narrative affects the mental, emotional, spiritual, and physical aspects of their being.

A personal narrative encompasses how these four life aspects are connected and how they affect each other. As a simple example: a young mother brought in her six-year-old son as a new patient. The major complaint for the visit was the boy's asthma. While there was nothing remarkable about the boy's history itself, his mother made a specific and interesting comment to me that forever changed the trajectory of my career and my life's work. She said, "I swear, it's almost as if my son can bring about an asthma attack on purpose."

That one comment stuck with me, throughout the remainder of the day and into the evening. It wasn't until later that night, when I awoke from a deep sleep, that I realized the importance of that comment. It hit me like a bolt of lightning—if he can bring on an asthma attack, can he also choose to stop it? That was the defining moment that put me on the path towards my current philosophy.

I realized there had to be a link between an individual's thought and their well-being. But it is not only thought or mental ideation for which this link exists. It is also the other mental, emotional, and physical aspects that affect well-being and health. Although that six-year-old boy was my first introduction to this lifelong journey, there was another pivotal event in my life that I can only call divine intervention.

I was lying in bed one night, praying, asking that I be shown the way in which I could dedicate my life to finding the connection between the human spirit and health. There is the adage, "Be careful what you wish for, you just might get it." And sometimes you get it in the form of something that is completely unexpected. That is what happened to me, and while at the time I certainly could not understand the importance of what was happening, today I see it as a gift and am incredibly grateful.

When I was 40 years old, a few weeks after my prayer intervention, I was working out at a local gym lifting weights. During one set of reps, I heard a click in my neck but thought nothing of it. As a chiropractor, I thought it was no big deal and if I needed to get an adjustment, that was easy enough to do. But after a few days, I started to have a funny feeling in my arm. Over the next couple weeks, it was getting worse, not better. I had numbness in my left shoulder and was now experiencing hand weakness as well.

I kept writing it off as a pulled muscle. The funny thing is the only thing being pulled was my EGO. I was still living my life as though this was no big deal and did not think much about the severity of my injury. Until one day I started experiencing severe pain. It was so bad that I, a chiropractor, went to an orthopedic doctor, who gave me some pain killers and sent me home. Again, I went back to thinking life was great.

But it wasn't. I woke up in severe pain. I was living by myself, and the pain killers were not working. It got so bad that I literally slammed myself into a wall, hoping to adjust the pain I was feeling in my shoulder and arm. Six weeks from the date of my initial injury at the gym, I found myself having emergency surgery on my neck. Unbeknownst to me at the time, I had ruptured discs C5 and C6. I needed a metal plate installed in my neck to address the injury I had sustained.

And just like that, in an instant, I was in practice one day, and then I had to face the realization that I was never going to be able to practice chiropractic medicine again. What was also VERY interesting was I now knew what a patient meant when they said, "I am in severe pain." Even though I had been a doctor for years, I never fully understood what my patients meant when they described their pain to me.

What an awakening of spirit this produced in me. That is how my passion began to thoroughly understand the human spirit and its connection to health. So, my prayers were answered-- but certainly not in the way I expected. Because I could no longer practice chiropractic medicine due to the weakness in my cervical vertebrae, I was therefore free to follow my passion to search and find the missing ingredient in our healthcare system.

As you learn about the Big Four Process, you'll see where it can fit into your belief system. And if you do not agree, that is also great! Everyone has a different personal narrative. I am not here to argue or judge what someone believes. But what I do know is the data and information I have from the years of treating thousands— and yes, I mean thousands— of patients. I had some very good results. The only thing that every human is guaranteed is that the moment you are born, you are going to die. Everyone dies. But what happens in between birth and death is unique for each person.

MISSION STATEMENT OF THE BIG FOUR PROCESS

To create and teach a Healing Art to save humanity, by understanding the connection of the spiritual, mental, emotional, and physical aspects as experienced and learned through The Big Four Process.

1

THE FOUR PRINCIPLES

I know that I am very excited about what the Big Four Process can do and I want to introduce it to you. There are two goals for this book. The first goal is creating a change in your life when you experience the Big Four Process. I want to help you start a new journey, regardless of where you are right now, that will enable you to go and do and choose whatever you want. I want you to be able to decide that you can create the life you want and desire-- and deserve! The second goal is after you experience the Big Four Process, together we can introduce this new healing art to the world so that more people can receive the benefits it will provide. There are four important principles you should understand.

The first principle is we are a four-part being, composed of spiritual, mental, emotional, and physical aspects. The spiritual aspect is the highest "vibration." which creates the mental image, a vibration that is lower than the spiritual one. The spiritual creates the emotional vibration, which is lower still on the vibrational scale; and then from the emotion we have final aspect, the physical, which is the lowest vibration of them all—the matter of which we and the universe are made.

The second principle is you must have a thought before anything can be accomplished in this world. Without thought, there is nothing. You cannot wake up tomorrow morning feeling depressed or happy without first having had a thought. And it is that thought that something that happens in your head, which produces the mental image, which produces the emotional aspect, which then alters the physical aspect.

The third principle is if you have blocks anywhere between the spiritual-mental-emotional-physical aspects, you cannot reach your potential, and be all that you can be. This will be demonstrated in the pages to follow.

The fourth aspect is the most important, because it is the critical element to you experiencing success with the Big Four Process! It is that your subconscious mind is going to find the blocks, not your conscious mind.

Okay, let's summarize the four principals before we move on. 1) We are a four-part being spiritual, mental, emotional, physical. 2) To achieve anything in this world you must first have a thought. 3) An obstacle in the form of a belief system can block any aspect of the Big Four Process: spiritual to mental to emotional to physical. 4) The subconscious finds the blocks, not the conscious mind.

What is a block? A block is a belief, usually a limiting idea, which is keeping you from achieving harmony and balance in your whole being. And this, in turn, prevents you from living the life you should live. An example of a spiritual block would be questioning why God allowed something "bad" to happen to my friend? Whereas a mental block would be expressed by statements like, "I cannot do that," or "I do not understand why I cannot make money." Emotional blocks, which are caused by false belief systems, sound like, "I hate my mother." Physical blocks are generally the easiest for most patients to understand because they relate to ailments or conditions they experience in their bodies, such as being overweight, or having fragile discs.

It is fascinating that in my experience of the patients I have treated, 95 percent of the time the real problem is not a defect in the physical body. Instead, it is a block in the spiritual, mental, or emotional which is being expressed in the physical body. What is exciting is that most of my patients have tried numerous other medical modalities and approaches. Often times they tell me they have literally tried everything they could think of. And because of this, they are ready for something new like the Big Four Process. And once they use the Big Four Process, they see results!

In this book, you will learn an example of how thought alone, altered the physical world after the horrific events of September 11th, 2001. You will also learn the sad story about Mr. Long, a gentleman who died of cancer because he was consumed by fear and thought that he was going to die. In a study involving the mental aspect, you will find out about the 6 second delay, which will change your understanding of the conscious and the subconscious mind.

One of the best parts about this experience is that some of the examples are my personal patients. You will learn about two of my patients, not a theoretical case study, but rather these were hands on personal experiences that I witnessed in my office. Both cases involve patients that came to me because they were overweight, and while only one patient lost physical weight, both patients are now happy as a result of going through the Big Four Process. Through the Big Four Process, we found the emotional and mental blocks.

When you read the story of the woman and the Hershey bar,

this involves a spiritual block she had due to a false belief. You will understand why the second patient is happy even though she did not lose any weight. The Big Four Process allowed the second patient to bring awareness to her situation at the spiritual, mental, emotional, and physical levels.

If the examples I just gave are not enough to intrigue you, there will be the story of Nick Stata who died because he thought he froze to death, even though he was never exposed to any temperature that was below freezing. In his false belief, he quite literally ended up blocking all four aspects of the Big Four Process. You will also learn about psychologist Ellen Langer, Ph.D., who headed a study from Harvard University, which demonstrates how changing a person's environment can change their physiology and thus change their physical aspect.

As I am writing this, I am in a coffee shop, and I am again reminded of the importance of you, the reader, because I want you to know there are ways to respond to negative situations and heal. I understand how difficult it is to stay healthy and balanced in the world that we live in today. By you reading this material, you probably understand already that health is not just taking a pill, nor is it just exercising, or eating healthy. Rather, it is the exploration of ALL of you— the spiritual, mental, emotional, and physical parts of you-- the Big Four Process. I appreciate and respect your commitment to your health and well-being. I once had a women complain to me that what she didn't like about the chiropractic approach is that you always have to go back! But where she missed the boat is in the belief that you always have to keep going back. When, in fact, a good life is not about the number of office visits you have to make, it is about improving your life on all levels, not just from the chiropractic viewpoint.

What I can say to you is that no matter what your situation is, the only constant in the universe is change. Therefore, once you experience the Big Four Process, you will be able to keep working on yourself. Because this process is like peeling the layers of an onion— there are always more layers, and with each layer you go deeper and get better and better results. You will have a different perception each time you do the Big Four Process, and in so doing, you will continue to improve and grow and remove blocks.

Have you ever read a book twice and thought to yourself, "I did not understand the first time, but now I get it?" The book didn't change, your perception did. Just like with the Big Four Process, you will change each time you do it. As you read the information presented in this book, I encourage you to experience, with an open mind not just with your intellect. You are a culmination of the results of all the experiences you have had, be they good, bad, or indifferent. This leads to your belief system, and this is all part of your personal narrative.

If you are struggling, or you are in pain, or you want a better life for yourself, now is your time to decide to change the patterns, find the blocks, and experience the health and the life you want. You can achieve this by using something new—the Big Four Process. You will experience a change that will bring you from where you stand right now, to anywhere you choose to go. It is time for you to step into your power and take control of your own life. You are in charge of yourself, nobody else is. It is important for you to understand this.

Neither your mother or father, nor husband, wife, brother, sister, friend, lover can help you achieve the results you want. YOU are the one who can help you. It's completely up to you with the Big Four Process.

Einstein is famous for saying, "We cannot solve our problems with the same thinking we used when we created them." If you focus on the problem, all that is present in that thought is the vibration, the echo of the problem. The solution is found when you look for answers to the problem, not just focusing on the problem itself. This is why it is useful for people to engage in other activities that will "get their mind off their problem." It allows the brain to shift the perception and in so doing, you can raise your vibration to the place where the solution can be found.

The Big Four Process will allow you to expedite this process of identifying a false belief that is creating a block and then eliminate it. It could be a false belief in any of the four aspects: spiritual, mental, emotional, or physical. This is the power of what the Big Four Process can do for you.

Think of an oak tree that starts as a small acorn. That one tiny acorn can grow up to 90 feet tall, weighing thousands of pounds and possess incredible strength. But if everyday someone nicks the bark of that oak tree, eventually it will become weak and unable to sustain itself, and it will die. Think of yourself as the oak tree. If, over the course of your lifetime, you suffer nicks in the form of spiritual blocks, emotional blocks, mental blocks and physical blocks, these nicks are slowly killing who you are.

I ask that you find a place where you can relax, be comfortable, take a deep breath, turn your devices off, and read this book with an open mind and an open heart. Find the space within that allows you to put yourself and your well-being first. I cannot promise it will be easy, I don't know what your path has been.

No matter what has happened in your life, no matter what level of physical health you may be experiencing now, I do know that balance is possible for you. I do know that everyone deserves happiness, and to live their best life. To be the strongest that they can be, the best they can be, and realize the joy in being a fully spiritual being having a human experience. People change either out of desperation or inspiration. It is my most sincere wish that you choose to change out of inspiration.

The Tiger and the Big Four Process

First, let us review the connection of the four aspects of The Big Four Process that we briefly covered in the introduction. It is vital that you understand The Big Four Process from the start. Let's use a tiger as our example for this overview. Bear with me, we'll get to people soon enough. Keep in mind as well that we will use the words *thought* and *spiritual* interchangeably.

For the First Aspect, think of a tiger, the big orange and black cat of the Asian jungles. What happens when you think "tiger?" You picture something, but maybe it's a favorite stuffed tiger you had when you were a child. Perhaps even a real-life encounter with a tiger at a zoo. The point is that you access a picture of something called "tiger" in your mind and at that point you begin the mental aspect of The Big Four Process.

As the thought enters the second aspect of The Big Four Process, the non-tangible thought starts to become tangible because now a mental picture is formed in your mind. From that quick hint of memory, now you begin to fill in the details and complete the image. You may recall a whole constellation of sensations describing your dream tiger. Perhaps you can feel the soft fur of the stuffed tiger and how it comforted you to clutch it when you were a small child. Maybe you feel instead a little thrill of fear from being so close to the real tiger pacing back and forth in its enclosure at the zoo, realizing that it was looking at you as you looked at it. Did you gaze into those huge golden eyes for just a moment and wonder what the tiger was seeing?

It's this mental picture of the tiger, soft and comforting or pacing and scary, that determines the third aspect, the emotional response that you will choose to experience. The emotions depend on how you process that mental picture, due to your past experiences. Is the emotion a peaceful nostalgia for a glimpse of happiness in childhood or is it a little tingle down your spine from looking into the eyes of an apex predator?

The last aspect of The Big Four Process, the physical, is conditioned by how you interpret that tiger. If all the tigers in your life have been cuddly stuffed animals, you will not have a negative emotional response to your mental image of a tiger. You know it is not a real tiger. Thus, it will not affect your physical aspect, your heart rate, or your respiration.

If you can recall an actual tiger, the situation will be vastly different. If you stood almost nose to nose with a real tiger, you will experience a fight or flight impulse. Depending on your experience, it may be mild or more pronounced. It can easily result in an altering of your physical body—a flutter in your heart rhythm, a bead of sweat on your forehead. All that from the momentary firing of a few neurons deep in your mind that respond to the idea—tiger.

Each of the next four chapters will cover one of the four aspects of the Big Four Process, with specific examples of each-- spiritual, mental, emotional, and physical. While some examples may appear to have an undetermined outcome in the common view of most people, the results were positive in the patients' perception. Let me emphasize here that each and every outcome takes its meaning from the patient's personal narrative and their individual interpretation based on their unique needs and expectations. Not all happy endings are the same.

To simplify the Big Four Process, I will use the ongoing hypothetical examples of four men-- Tom, Bob, Randy, and John-- all of whom chose to stop smoking using the Big Four

Process. Obviously, each of these men—let's call them our lab rats-- had a unique life narrative up to the point of the Big Four Process intervention, but it is important to understand that each also had his own reasons for wanting to quit and his own specific expectations of how this would improve his life and relationships going forward.

2

SPIRITUAL ASPECT OF THE BIG FOUR PROCESS

What is a thought? A thought is something that has no weight, no volume. You cannot see it or smell it or even feel it. It is the highest vibration known to man. But before we get into that question, let's stop for a moment to talk about what we mean by "vibration." We will use this concept often in the following discussions, so let's agree on what it means for our purposes here.

"Vibration" is really a term of convenience for something we are all familiar with, but neither the layperson nor the scientist can define it precisely. We use it in this book to mean that firing of some array of neurons deep in your brain that allows you to have a thought or to make a movement or to react to a tune or the color of a person's eyes, to fetch a memory from years ago or feel the excitement of just this instant in time. It is a passage of energy reacting with the physical matter of your brain and the rest of your nervous system. It creates what we commonly call thought.

We call this a "vibration" and take our cue from the prevailing theory of physics—string theory. In this theory, all the particles that make up matter are ultimately vibrating strings. Every vibration has a harmonic that creates our reality. If vibrations are the basis of our universe, as string theory contends, then this seems like a good term to designate those invisible, infinitesimal but powerful events that trigger our thoughts and move us through life.

You will read more about vibrations as we continue. Meanwhile, back to our question—what is a thought? Gallons of ink have been spilled debating the answer, but for our purposes here, a thought is an idea or an opinion about a particular topic. Thinking is the process of using one's mind to create a reason or a realization about some thing or event. Science does not know where thoughts come from, or how the brain receives or manufactures a thought. But that is OK for our purposes.

In this book, we are not going to discuss the origin of thought. What is important is to discuss how the human body is both electrical and magnetic in nature and how thoughts, however they are generated, move through our body and our being and shape our lives, and our own perception of our life. This will be demonstrated throughout the book with studies in each of the four aspects, spiritual, mental, emotional, and physical.

In the last few decades, researchers have used both functional Magnetic Resonance Imaging (fMRI) and Positron Emission Tomography (PET) to study how the actions of our neurons generate detectable electric fields inside our brain tissue. Using these tools, it is actually possible to see thoughts happening inside the brain and various parts of the brain literally "lighting up" as a thought develops. The thought remains intangible, but we can see what we might call the vibrations happening as it passes from one group of neurons to the next.

Why is a thought intangible? We can see the vibration in an fMRI or a PET scan, but we cannot measure it. We can't weigh it.

We can't see what color it is. We know it's there by its energy and movement, but is that enough?

As I created the Big Four Process, one question that came up constantly is-- how scientific is it? I respond that today's science is amazing, but it is also a work in progress. At the heart of the scientific method is this idea—all conclusions are contingent. I am working in an area where our technical knowledge has many gaps, and these gaps make it difficult for us to address many life conditions which do not have an obvious physical basis. We are particularly good at healing broken bones or defeating known pathogens (bacteria, viruses, fungi) where we can test and measure down to the nearest microgram.

But many of the conditions that you and I encounter that make people unhappy, leave them in pain, prevent them from functioning and participating fully in life do not have at their core little beasties like bacteria that we can track down and attack. Those are the maladies that I try to address with the Big Four Process approach.

All our minds and bodies have at their core an energy that the medical world calls "homeostasis." Homeostasis is the mechanism inside everybody, every cell, every life that tries to keep running on an even keel. Homeostasis is like a combination of autocorrect and GPS; when functioning well, it keeps us on the right path in terms of basic functions. It keeps us from veering off the road and into the ditch every day in every little aspect of living.

We can call this life energy God or homeostasis. Even though where it comes from or exactly how it works is largely unknown, we all would agree that a thought—a normal, everyday thought or a big, life altering thought-- can alter the physical body as it goes to the four phases we named earlier—mental, emotional, physical, and spiritual. As we noted in our example of the tiger, it can raise your blood pressure or lower your blood pressure, depending on your body or mental image.

The following four examples focus on the supreme power of thought; how thought itself can affect everything, sometimes even bypassing the other aspects such as mental and emotional with a potential combination of good and bad results.

The First Example: 911

The first example of the power of thought is unique. It demonstrates the power of thought through the group consciousness of an entire country. Most Americans remember the exact place and time where they were on September 11, 2001, when almost three thousand individuals died due to the terrorist attack on the World Trade Center. On that day, Americans were united emotionally with grief and outrage.

Now look what happened one year later on September 11, 2002. One year after September 11, 2001, the lottery numbers chosen for the Pick-3 lottery in New York City on September 11, 2002, was "911." Was it a coincidence or was it due to a large number of people all thinking of 911? Did all those thoughts, many of them certainly intense and heartfelt, affect the lottery, in the number 911 being drawn on that day one year later, despite the lottery's elaborately "untouched by human hands" random number process? Obviously, this cannot be measured scientifically, but it may have value in our ongoing investigation of "The Big Four Process."

If thoughts are electrical but cannot be measured outside the human skull, how did this incident occur? We can assume that the thoughts of people in America and all over the world, who were affected by the events of the day, in person or by accounts in the news, all focused on the same mental images. Millions of people all over the world, all having a mental image of the falling towers, the huge plumes of smoke and ash, the hundreds and thousands of desperate people fleeing down the streets of Manhattan may have created a collective consciousness that made an electrical footprint that subtly touched the whirling numbered balls in the lottery's carefully calibrated machine.

Pause for a moment and try to recall exactly where you were and what you felt that September morning. It only takes a moment for most of us to hear those terrible words, see the incredible destruction in our mind's eye, to be in that thrilling instant again. How does that move you? How do you feel it? Powerful even after more than twenty years, right? What could all of that surging energy do on that terrible anniversary? Tipping three little plastic balls ever so slightly doesn't feel like too much of a stretch, does it?

Four Minute Mile

Our second example, the legendary four-minute mile, also demonstrates how a group consciousness can affect one person individually—and vice-versa. Your physical ability can actually shift because someone else completed a task once thought to be impossible. In the world of competitive running, there was an obsession to break the four-minute mile. The best runners in the world attempted this feat repeatedly after WW II, but to no avail. Even using the latest knowledge of running physiology and the improved running shoes then available, no man could break that four-minute barrier.

It was finally accomplished by Roger Bannister on May 6, 1954, who ran the four-minute mile in 3 minutes and 59.4 seconds. After Bannister broke the four-minute mile, consciousness shifted. Runners, who had not changed physically, who were using the same shoes, eating the same diet suddenly knew that breaking the four-minute barrier was possible. John Landy also broke the four-minute mile a few weeks after Bannister.

What occurred was when one person, Roger Bannister, broke that seemingly unconquerable barrier, he demonstrated to other individuals with a similar personal narrative: "If I could do it, so can you." By changing the first aspect, thought, Bannister raised the consciousness of every athlete. The impossible was now possible and new goals were set by runners to beat the new record.

The runners did not change. The mile track didn't change. Stop watches didn't change. Only the idea changed—and barriers fell one after another. Today the one-mile sprint record stands at 3:43.13. That's a real time measured by the best electronic clocks in the sport, but it's also an idea just waiting to be challenged and changed by the power of the human mind.

Sam Long

Let's look at another example of how a negative thought based on a false belief can have surprising consequences. A fellow by the name of Sam Long was a retired shoe salesperson—about as ordinary a background as you can find, a regular guy, most of us would say. Back in 1970, six months after Sam lost his wife of many years, he found himself feeling less and less well. One doctor led to another which led to tests and X-rays. Finally, a doctor told Sam he had a metastatic throat cancer. The cancer had spread to the left lobe of his liver. In 1970, this was effectively a death sentence.

After that burst of bad luck, Sam met a woman who fell for him, despite his terrible prognosis. Perhaps love is blind, or maybe it sees further and deeper. The gracious lady offered to care for him throughout his illness, so they married and moved to Nashville. In Nashville, through another twist of fate, Sam came under the care of oncologist, Dr. Clifton Medle. During a hospital visit, Dr. Medle thoughtfully asked Sam, "What do you want from your remaining days." Sam explained that he wanted to live long enough to experience one more Christmas with his new wife and her family, to have this one last taste of happiness.

Dr. Medle promised to do his best to get Sam through the balance of that year. Surprisingly, over the course of the weeks and months leading up to Christmas, Sam began showing substantial improvements, which amazed Dr. Medle, as well as Sam and his new wife. Sam made it through Christmas, and by all indications, his health had taken an unexpected turn for the better. Then, unexpectedly, Sam died on New Year's Eve. But that's not the end of the story.

Sam's autopsy revealed a completely unexpected turn of events. His liver had a much smaller tumor than was originally seen in the diagnostic tests. His liver function was not impaired, and the remaining tumor did not contribute to his death. Moreover, his throat cancer had completely disappeared. Sam was almost cancer free.

If the cancer did not kill Sam, what did? The final autopsy report listed the cause of death as undetermined. Is it possible that Sam Long died, not from a medical condition that could be found on an autopsy table, but rather because he deeply believed that he was going to die right after Christmas? It's a well-known fact that death rates in the US spike at Christmas and the day after a New Year. This puzzle has been commented on by epidemiologists for years. But that's in the US. In Asia, the same thing happens the day after the Lunar New Year! So, what is the role of thought, those vibrations we talk about, in terms of bodily heath? Can we literally think ourselves dead?

This example leads us forward to important discussions about the role of thought, healing, and disease.

Larry and Aids

Our last example for the spiritual aspect is the story of a person we'll call Larry, to protect his privacy. You will discover why in a moment. Larry chose to turn away from false beliefs which were blocking his mental, emotional, and physical aspects in a dangerous way. In my years of experience in working with many different people, I have come to the conclusion that people change—if they change—either out of inspiration or desperation. I think Larry changed out of desperation but draw your own conclusion.

Larry was an African American gay man with AIDS. This was some years ago when AIDS was far more dangerous than it is now. Keep that in mind.

Larry was told by his physician that he had only three months to live. Years back, this was not uncommon with AIDS. But here's an important condition—Larry had been brought up in a strongly religious family. God had been an intimate part of his life from childhood on. He thought in fundamentally spiritual terms, saw the world as a place infused with spirit, not just a random collection of soulless people surrounded by mere material things.

Not surprisingly, Larry had lived in a state of constant conflict in his personal narrative. He was gay, and yet in his religious beliefs, being gay was fundamentally wrong. Between his infection with AIDS and his deep internal conflict, the odds did not look good for Larry—but let us see what actually happened. After all, probability is not destiny.

Conventional medicine at that time had little more to offer, so Larry made a reconciliation of the spirit, his primary treatment mode. He incorporated the concepts of the Big Four Process with his spiritual upbringing in ingenious ways. Larry changed his hospital room to make it what he thought of as a "place touched by God." He drew on every aspect of his culture and his religious upbringing to focus on his healing. The center of his belief now became a visualization of recovery, of the intense joy of a life without AIDS.

For many of us, this brings up a question about God. Did God actually touch Larry, intervene in his journey towards healing? We can't really know of course, but we do know that Larry's strong belief focused his own energies on recovery. In the context of Larry's personal narrative as a believer, such intervention was entirely possible. As a lifelong member of a strong African American church, immersed in both a family and a community of fellow believers, Larry had fully internalized the idea of the world as a place of the spirit where prayer and grace are as real as the weather. When talking about the power of the mind, we have to be open to the idea that a deep belief in grace may bring grace about in ways not subject to CAT scans and lab tests.

I once heard Dr. Bernie Siegel say that there are no incurable diseases only incurable patients. This is an especially important statement. Larry did not want to die, he wanted to live and that was half the battle. You may object that we all want to live, but for many of us that's really only true if it's not too much work, if we don't have to struggle, bear pain, push past all of the black thought that can pull us down. For the second half of his battle, Larry strengthened his personal narrative by calling upon his early religious, biblical, spiritual formation, and education. He designed a personal intervention to beat the medical odds.

Larry believed the Bible was a tool for empowerment and strength, even though others might interpret the Bible in a negative way, as no more than a list of "thou shalt not" commands. He did not see himself as a victim, even though he realized that some people might use the Bible to reject his homosexuality. This patient knew that on some level all humans have free will, and at the same time, the results of their decisions cannot be changed. It is possible that Larry understood that God gives a person an alternative to their situations; since a person cannot change what happens to them, they can change only the way they feel about it. That is what Larry did.

How Larry created the Big Four Process in another way was that he created a special hospital room, which became God's home to him. Larry called friends to pray with him with the requests of believers, no pity parties, no begging, spiritual warriors only, individuals who know God. The participants would circle his bed in the hospital and go into deep prayer. Larry had an herbalist who treated the physical aspect of "The Big Four Process," a therapist who treated the mental aspect, and an acupuncturist who worked on the emotional aspect.

The result was beyond expectations or explanation. Gradually, Larry recovered. His AIDS went into what the doctors call spontaneous remission. Larry's is but one story of many. Can we think our way healthy? There is an age-old saying that chance favors the prepared mind. We tend to think that, even with all of our modern medical technology, health may favor the willing spirit.

3

MENTAL ASPECT OF THE BIG FOUR PROCESS THE BIG FOUR PROCESS

We are now going to explore the second component of the Big Four Process, "The Mental Aspect." This is extremely exciting to me because this is where the rubber meets the road, where we discover a new understanding of how the Big Four Process works. This exploration is based on what I have learned from being a clinician and researcher over the past 40 years.

I initially wondered why the second phase of the Big Four Process would be a mental image. The individual first has a thought and then a mental image is produced. During my doctoral research, I came across a vital clue in Jeanne Achterberg's book *Imagery in Healing*. Achterberg feels that when you have a thought, the thought must be turned into an actionable mental image. The mental image should be a symbol which is understood by the individual. Partial or fragmentary images are assembled into a more complete mental image or symbol. This symbol is then communicated to the person's inner self, or subconscious.

This is an important finding in The Big Four Process because we are dealing with the clearing of subconscious needs and wants. We will discuss in a later chapter why this is critical when you begin to work with the seven mental cards we'll use as aids to discovery. For the moment, this glance ahead is just a teaser, but rest assured that we'll be showing you how to make very practical use of these concepts later in this discussion.

In deploying The Big Four Process, we are not changing the underlying thought, which produces the mental image, instead we are creating a new meaning for the mental image. The Big Four Process changes your negative false belief into a new positive belief by changing your perceptions of the existing situation and reimagining what it means.

Remember that Einstein said no problem can be solved on the same vibration in which it was created. In stressing the empowerment of the individual, we are helping everyone reading this book to make better decisions. These better decisions will only feel right for the individual when they change the *meaning* of the mental image, but NOT BY CHANGING THE image itself. Given how intimately thoughts create the unconscious images, which would almost be impossible. When the individual listens to their inner self and understands their personal narrative, they will also have an increased understanding of their body's needs and their well-being.

We talk about decisions quite often. Keep in mind this fundamental truth. Your life is nothing more than the sum total of the decisions you have made over the years. Yes, outside events impact your life—but your decisions about how to react to and deal with those events determine how they shape your life going forward. Think back and ask yourself—and answer honestly—how much of the "bad luck' in your life has been caused by or made worse by poor decisions on your part? At its heart, the Big Four Process is simply a mental discipline to help you make consistently better decisions by understanding your inner decision process as it moves through what we call its "aspects."

The following example of changing the meaning of the image comes from two of my patients. I had a single parent bring his two children to my office. The parents were divorced when the boy was fifteen and the girl was twelve. Each child had a negative image of the divorce, not at all unusual. It does not matter what the specific image is, what is important is the meaning of the image.

Divorce to the children means what? It means dealing with questions like, "Will I see daddy (or mommy) on Christmas, or will I only see him (or her) on weekends?" "Do I have to choose who I live with?" And many more comparable questions, all of them requiring wrenching decisions by both the parents and the children. After using the Big Four Process and discovering the false beliefs in their spiritual, mental, emotional, and physical aspects, both patients were able to intentionally change the meaning of the images in their mental aspect.

In a meditation, I used a little trick to surface the hidden images that were confusing the children's decisions. I posed an alternate reality; what if the family all stayed together somehow, but were all killed in a subsequent plane crash? Would they prefer that, over where they are now? If the person has to choose life over death, most people will choose life. Even more to the point in this case, thinking about ultimate loss helped each person think through the blessings that remained in spite of the divorce. Yes, divorce can be terrible, but if you can still hug your parents and tell them you love them, still have holidays and other special times together, you can use those images to make better decisions about how to cherish what remains and lessen the bitterness of what has been lost.

Shakespeare tells us that, "There is nothing good or bad but thinking makes it so." What was more important to this family—

the tragedy of the divorce or the joy of so many, many years of life and love still left for them to make the most of? The point of our Big Four Process is to help you make the best decisions regardless of the curveball's life throws your way.

When I think of the mental aspect of The Big Four Process, a particular memory comes to me. While working on my doctorate. I remember that one way I used to demonstrate the mental aspect of the Big Four Process was to use a lemon. I told the class to close their eyes and picture a lemon. Picture that you are cutting the lemon into slices. You slowly raise a lemon slice to your mouth, and you are going to bite into it. You will start to produce saliva. Then the professor teaching the class said that my example was unacceptable because salivating was merely conditioning, like Pavlov's dogs. Obviously, the professor thought dogs don't have a level of mental awareness. New research suggests they do—but I digress.

What I was attempting to demonstrate is that if a person is thinking of a lemon, that person will have the mental image of the lemon, therefore, creating the emotional response of sourness in the last aspect of the Big Four Process, the physical, and produce a physiological reaction-- salivating. I could not sleep that night because of what the professor said. I knew I was right-- not because I needed to be right, but because of my past clinical experience. I knew I needed a different example of the power of the mental aspect. During the night, the perfect example dawned on me—hypnosis. So, a few days later, I had three examples ready, where a thought creates a mental image to produce a physical change.

Three Examples of Hypnosis

Study One: This small study investigated a fairly simple question. If a normal person is put under hypnosis and then told that they are developing an ordinary blister—the kind you get when a shoe is too tight—will any of them actually develop a visible blister? This is a good question because a blister is obvious. It can be seen and palpated, and a real blister will run a predictable course from initial appearance though healing. There is nothing subjective about a blister. Out of twenty-one subjects, none of which had a blister, fourteen developed a blister in direct response to the suggestion under hypnosis. Pavlovian? I think not.

Interestingly, many studies of hypnosis itself have shown that about three quarters of a random group of people will be susceptible to hypnotic suggestion in some degree. Hypnosis is, of course, a purely mental procedure. The hypnotized person is in an altered mental state in which the mind is unusually receptive to thoughts induced by the hypnotist. While this experiment opens up a large area for further discussion, our only interest here is the clear way in which it shows how mere thought can alter the physical body.

Study Two: In another study, thirty children with leukemia and non-Hodgkin's lymphoma, were divided into two groups. One group was hypnotized and given direct suggestions which would be associated with managing the pain from the lumbar punctures (or spinal tap) involved in their course of treatment. The second group was given indirect hypnotic suggestions involving their lumbar punctures. The question was not whether hypnosis could impact the course of the underlying disease. Rather it looked at whether hypnosis could help the patients to manage the considerable pain involved in this particular clinical procedure.

The experiment demonstrated a significant statistical reduction from the baseline for pain. It also demonstrated a reduction in anxiety during a lumbar puncture which was evident in both groups. Bear in mind, the patients are all children, so reducing pain and anxiety is especially desirable. In this study, both groups experienced positive results through nothing more than believing, because of the hypnotic suggestion, that it would not hurt as much. This example illustrates in overly dramatic terms how thought effects well-being.

Study Three: In an article in *Science Direct,* "Hypnosis for Burn Wound Care Pain and Anxiety: A Systematic Review and Meta-Analysis," the authors point out that in many medical procedures, hypnosis not only plays a role in reducing pain, but also reduces emotional distress. They point out that hypnosis can improve recovery, stabilize physiological parameters, and reduce procedural time. This indicates that the thoughts of a patient can stimulate a change in the physical body and can alter aspects of the personal narrative by reducing emotional stress.

Why does hypnosis affect the personal narrative, the Big Four Process, and well-being? One reason that hypnosis works is that during the process of being hypnotized, a disorientation is created which produces an inhibitory process within the conscious mind. Basically, hypnosis bypasses the individual's analytic mind that uses the facts and knowledge accumulated over the years to make decisions. Some number of these recollections support false beliefs. During the process of being hypnotized, the individual is letting down all their defense mechanisms, becoming highly responsive to suggestions layered into their subconscious mind.

As the individual's conscious mind is held in abeyance, the subconscious mind has the freedom to absorb new information. As we continue to demonstrate the second aspect of the Big Four Process, the mental, we need to discuss the role that the subconscious plays in the mental aspect of the Big Four Process. This is where false beliefs known as blocks develop.

The Subconscious and Well-Being

I cannot stress enough how important The Big Four Process is to understand what happens in the mind. There is a difference between remembering something and understanding something. It is so important to understand it now, while you can use this discipline to live a better life and find a better future. By reading this book, you are ahead of ninety percent of the people around you. Most people are followers and are afraid to move on with new knowledge due to fear of growth or the unknown.

The subconscious mind has complete knowledge and awareness of every system in your body and encompasses all the many functions that are not under conscious control. Think of all the activities going on in your body at any given moment. You are digesting your last meal, regulating your breathing, adjusting your heart rate to whatever tasks you have in hand. Beyond that, your sense of balance is keeping you upright, your eyes and ears are keeping track of what's going on, even when you are not consciously paying attention. Even the hairs on the back of your neck are picking up signals from the air moving around you. Your sense of smell is much sharper than you realize because it operates unconsciously most of the time.

Your brain is absolutely buzzing with more activities than we can easily list, but only a few get to your conscious mind. Everything else is going on in your subconscious—unless something happens that sends an alarm signal to the conscious brain. If you're a new mother, for example, your subconscious will hear your baby's faintest cry two rooms away and ring your alarm bells instantly. Our conscious mind is smart, but our subconscious is astounding.

The subconscious mind can absorb millions of bits of sensory information from the nervous system every second. It can process forty million bits of data per second which is running ninety five percent of your daily activity. The subconscious mind is stronger than the conscious mind. The subconscious mind encompasses the awareness of all activities that the conscious mind does not choose to recognize. The subconscious mind is motivated by duty, not desire or enthusiasm. In my research, this is the one statement that has the most value in discovering how the Big Four Process works, how personal narrative affects one's well-being. This is because the subconscious does not know what is right or wrong, what is good or bad, or even what is positive or negative in the individual's life. The goal of the subconscious is to protect the individual based on its understanding of life initially created from birth to seven years old. This is an especially important observation because it explains why individuals make choices that only makes sense to themselves and not to other individuals.

The subconscious mind can only respond to what the conscious mind imprints on it, based on its unique experiences. The individual's subconscious mind will never sabotage the person. It simply operates based on whatever was imprinted in the past, either good or bad. The subconscious mind does not know how to sabotage the individual, even if the individual has a conscious awareness that he/she would like to change a situation.

This is a major observation because it explains why some individuals cannot move forward in their personal narrative and well-being due to the way they unconsciously programmed a negative false belief, however many years ago. As an example, if an individual says that he or she wants to lose weight because they know that being overweight is an unhealthy choice, it may be difficult for them to stop overeating, depending on how their personal narrative (the Big Four Process) was affected by their past experiences and family history.

In my practice, I saw many patients experiencing this situation. When an individual chooses to lose weight, only five percent of the personal narrative resides in the conscious mind. Deep inside the subconscious lurk all those memories from childhood: Clean your plate, think of the starving children in China, I made this just for you, it's your favorite (so, of course, you eat the whole thing), don't be picky, your father worked hard to make the money to buy food for you. All those subconscious memories sabotage the resolutions of your conscious mind.

No matter what you are attempting to do-- lose weight, stop smoking, exercise, find a partner, make money, or even to learn to drive as a teenager-- you need to move from the first aspect of the Big Four Process, thought, to the second aspect, the mental, before you can get to the emotional and physical aspects.

The following is a perfect personal example of how to change the mental image and achieve success. I had a patient who was overweight, and our major finding was that growing up as a child, she was always rewarded with cake from her mom to keep her busy when she was being bad. This experience occurred when she was young, before she had developed an analytical mind. Therefore, this patient created a false belief system—that food represents love-- that was hindering her life. She was on a downward dive until we did the Big Four Process. She had a false belief that to be rewarded in life, you have to do something bad. Her relationships were a mess, she couldn't hold down a job, plus other problems.

It is exceedingly difficult to change that mental image of cake as a reward, buried deep in her subconscious, which negatively conditioned the third aspect of the Big Four Process, emotional. In this case, until the patient understood what caused her being overweight, her inability to have a healthy relationship with food, she could diet all she wanted, and it would not work long term. Her constant failures to control her eating triggered ongoing bouts of depression, which had to be addressed first.

Doing otherwise is like giving a patient with Chronic Obstructive Pulmonary Disease (COPD) bottled oxygen, expecting to fix the COPD.

I once gave a lecture at a hospital to a group of people diagnosed with ongoing, chronic depression. The ostensible causes of their depression ranged from death of a loved one to sexual abuse. There was one woman in the group who had no interest at all in the complementary healing modalities I was presenting. She stated that patients are not responsible for their health. She said, "I am clinically depressed because I have the blood work to prove it." She said that her son was killed in an auto accident at an early age.

Now I knew that a blood test had been devised quite recently which can detect the chemical indicators of certain types of depression, so I asked her a simple question, "Did you become depressed the very day your son was killed in the car accident?" A quick response of "Yes, of course." My next question was also quite simple, "If your blood had been taken and analyzed right after you heard about your son's death, would it have shown a clinical depression profile?" Obviously, the answer is "No."

My question is, "What came first, the positive blood test, or the change in the personal narrative for the Big Four Process?" Was it due to the continuously thinking and living in the state of depression, which alters the blood chemical composition to lead to a diagnosis of depression?"

While a tragic incident that triggers the development of clinical depression can happen in an instant—like a car crash—grief does not become ongoing depression severe enough to be traced in a blood test in that same instant. It has to work on the mind over time, to create a new personal narrative which traps the person in a downward spiral into the depressive state.

Validation of the Mental Aspect

The following will demonstrate how thought, which is 100% intangible, converts into a lower vibration which can be measured. The following study will demonstrate how you think you are making your decisions in your life, when your subconscious is really making the decisions, not you. It is called the seven second delay in which investigates the validity of the second aspect of the Big Four Process. This research will demonstrate the shift from a non-tangible thought to a mental image which can be measured scientifically. To rephase it, this research demonstrates how an intangible thought starts to enter the tangible world and can be measured. Therefore, it is possible that it can alter the physical body depending on your thoughts.

The study is from Germany, and it demonstrated that the brain decides what action the body will take seven seconds before the body knows what action it will take. In this research study in Germany, participants were asked to push a button with either their left or right hand. During the study, the participants had a fMRI scanning their brain. By observing the activities of the micro patterns in the frontopolar cortex of the brain, the researchers could predict seven seconds before the subject became aware of their decision, which hand they were going to use to push the button. What is important here is that if the brain knows seven seconds before the body does, then the subconscious is pulling the strings.

With the Big Four Process, you can reprogram the subconscious to connect the heart to the head. This is because between birth and seven years old, you are programing your subconscious mind. After seven years old, you start to form the analytical mind. This is when your conscious mind states something like, "I am going to stop eating chocolate," but a week later, you are still eating chocolate. This is because of a false belief, that you created between birth and seven years old. Your subconscious mind is controlling you because of something that happen between birth and seven years old. Even though it is a false belief, your subconscious is in control. Because your subconscious mind is here to protect you, it does not know right or wrong, positive, or negative; it just protects you based on all those lessons learned in early childhood. Because it is ninety-five percent in control, it is usually a losing battle for your conscious mind to override what the subconscious "knows."

With the Big Four Process, you now have a way to change an old false belief formed in the subconscious to a new belief reformed in your subconscious mind, which now connects the heart to the mind. Therefore, it only makes sense that if a person is thinking of depression every day, then that person will develop all the indices of depression.

Oxana Malaya - No Love

This example demonstrates what a child would do to be loved. Oxana Malaya was born in Ukraine in 1983. Oxana is internationally known because of how she was raised from the ages of three to seven, the time when the brain is developing. Malaya has been the subject of interviews, documentaries, and tabloid headlines for her dog-imitating behavior as a feral child. She was raised by dogs. Malaya was a normal child at birth according to medical records and doctors. At the age of three, she was neglected by her alcoholic parents and was left outside one night. Being alone outside at three years old, Malaya found comfort with the family dogs. When Malaya was found by the authorities, she was seven years old. Malaya could not talk and lacked the basic human skills, physically behaving like a dog; running on all fours, sleeping on the floor, barking instead of speaking, eating like a dog, and her hygiene was that of a dog.

Malaya's personal narrative was distorted due to her experiences from ages three to seven due to the lack of connection between her and her parents. A child's brain is very active-- "as many as one million new neural connections are formed every second." During her lack of human connection, Malaya was a child starving for love and attention. Due to her experiences, her brain development and personal narrative were altered from those of a normal child during early stages of life. Some authorities may say that Malay's situation was more about staying alive then attention for love.

There is another major effect on the mental aspect that you can change. It is the power that you hold in every word you speak. Due to my experience over decades of hands-on procedures with chiropractic care which included touching and communicating with thousands of patients, I experienced an energetic connection with my patients. In turn, I came to realize that an individual's voice has power, this was confirmed when I researched my thesis of THOUGHT affecting well-being.

Be careful what you say, you might experience it. I noticed that many of my patients would respond to my voice instead of their own voice. If I would say to a patient, "You will be in more pain tomorrow," most would be in more pain. If I would say, "This procedure may cause a little discomfort," most of them felt discomfort because they responded to what I told them. Over time, I learned to never ask a patient, "Are you still in pain?" because it gave certain patients an opportunity to complain, even though they might have been feeling better. Instead, I modified the question that I asked to, "How much improvement do you have?"

I realized that the patient's personal power, in reference to their THOUGHT, diminished because they lost their ability to think for themselves when they deferred to the doctor in the white coat. Because of this, one of the aspects of thought was altered due to outside influences on the patient. These influences are all around us-- living in a family that complains about everything, a family that experiences various diseases, constant advertisements to get a flu shot during flu season, a religious belief, or other past experiences, create and direct our THOUGHTS.

Death by Acronym

Mere words can kill a patient because of the way the patient misunderstands the words spoken. As a group of medical students were making hospital rounds in a cardiac ward, they came upon a patient hooked up to monitors. A doctor told them that the patient was suffering from "TS." When the students left this patient, the patient's monitors demonstrated a great deal of distress by an increased pulse rate, otherwise clear lungs filled up with fluid, and other symptoms.

When questioned by a nurse about what was upsetting this patient, a medical student said that the distinguished doctor said that it was a "Terminal Situation." The nurse assured the student that there must have been a misunderstanding because it was not a terminal situation. The patient had a minor problem called "tricuspid stenosis." The patient also heard what the doctor said, "TS," and she also thought she had a terminal situation. By nightfall, the patient died from acute heart failure.

Although this case does not provide details about the patient's history, the patient's personal narrative must have played a role in her unexplained death. Possibly, a family member had died of a heart attack, and she believed that was also her fate. Due to her personal narrative, what she believed altered her body and she passed away even though her minor clinical situation should have been non-fatal.

A Head Case

To clarify "being in your head," from my professional experiences, is when an individual did not fulfill the connection of all four aspects of the personal narrative, The Big Four Process: mental, emotional, physical, and spiritual. When the individual completes all four stages, they will move out of their head to their heart. That is what some complementary healing arts refer to as the heart-mind connection, moving from the head thinking to the heart, embedding the new idea in the entire body.

There is a force of the subconscious mind that is so powerful that it can stop an individual from smoking, or conversely, it can keep the individual smoking. Due to an individual's subconscious programming during their first seven years of life, either negative or positive, events can create a subconscious program about unhealthy habits, even smoking.

This can happen because the subconscious has no understanding if something is negative or positive. The ninety-five percent, which is the subconscious, runs the programs in the brain created by past experiences. These programs are also known as habits, which can create a dysfunction in the perception of well-being. Creating some type of "-olic" such as a shopaholic, alcoholic, chocoholic, or even workaholic.

We now are going to move on to the third aspect of The Big Four Process, the emotional. It may still be difficult to understand the principle of the Big Four Process. As you learn about the next two aspects, the emotional and physical, it may be easier for you to understand the power of the Big Four Process, and how you can change your life by changing your subconscious.

4

EMOTIONAL ASPECT OF THE BIG FOUR PROCESS

Before we enter the third aspect of The Big Four Process, the emotional, let's have a short review of the first two. Recall that the first aspect is a thought which is a vibration that has no weight or volume. You can't feel it or smell it, but that little pulse of energy in your brain will become a reality in the physical world. Every thought is conditioned by your personal belief system, your subconscious, and the truth of your lived experience.

Next, you enter the second aspect, the mental. Here the thought produces a mental image, a lower, less ephemeral vibration, so the thought can be experienced in the physical world.

Now here is the major point. The next step, into the third aspect, the emotional, will be embodied in the images and desires of your subconscious mind, your deeply personal narrative. It will not translate into the language of your conscious mind, of your overt wants and intentions. Here's a quick example to underline the difference. I had a patient who loved to be pitied by other people. He basked in expressions of pity, but he could not understand why when this was clearly a dysfunctional desire. In fact, he would unconsciously sabotage any opportunities that came to him, earning ever more pity from his circle of friends. What we discovered by using the Big Four Process was that in his personal narrative, deep in his subconscious, going back to a terrible early childhood, he equated pity with love. In courting pity, he fulfilled his human need for love. This is not as odd as you might think. The great Spanish poet, Miguel de Unamuno, observed, "To love with the spirit is to pity, and he who pities most loves most." But even though pity and love are closely related, courting failure to ensure pity was a seriously dysfunctional approach to life.

The third aspect, the emotional, is where the non-tangible thought becomes more tangible as the mental picture produces an emotion, an internal experience. The mental image, drawn from the person's deep narrative, will determine what emotion will be expressed and thus pass into the last phase, the Physical, which, in turn, can express itself in a broad range of forms from overt actions to events which are hidden inside the body, but which still have a powerful impact of the person's life and health.

As we begin our exploration of the third aspect, the emotional, it is important to recall that the human body is enveloped in an electromagnetic field. The first two aspects are electrical in nature, pulses of energy. The initiating thought and the mental image that flow from it exist only as electro-chemical events in a network of neurons in our brain. I believe that some immaterial force which we can conceptualize as God's energy enters a human as an intangible thought and that mere vibration becomes matter by going through the mental and emotional aspects first before it enters the physical.

Our electromagnetic field plays a key role in how our personal narrative shapes events and outcomes. Our emotions and physical activities generate bursts of electro-magnetic energy which can be detected and traced in a laboratory. We can see them as squiggly lines on a piece of graph paper. A neurologist can examine these lines and determine whether we are "normal." But, the neurologist cannot look at those lines and say whether our perceptions and actions in the world are correct or severely dysfunctional.

Here is an example of how our individual electromagnetic fields can interact with a major emotional event. The United States of America has two satellites called GOES, Geosynchronous Environmental Satellites, located in the northern and southern hemispheres. The purpose of these satellites is to monitor fluctuations in the earth's magnetic field. Throughout the years, the data falls within a range that is normal for the magnetic field of the earth. This all changed on September 11, 2001. On that date, scientists witnessed a spike in the magnetic field that they had never seen before.

With further investigation, scientists realized that the first occurred 15 minutes after the first plane hit the World Trade Center. A second study of the data, at Princeton University, confirmed the initial findings. One Princeton researcher believes that when the towers were hit, so many people around the world were affected in some way that the collective mental energy altered the normal magnetic fluctuations. We should note that these findings were produced by The Global Consciousness Project and are considered controversial by many in the scientific world.

Keep that in mind while we look at something you're very close to—the red blood cells circulating in your body right now. In the 1930's, researchers found that hemoglobin, which is rich in iron, a strongly magnetic element, has magnetic properties that vary with the amount of oxygen the blood is carrying. Hemoglobin's attachment to oxygen is affected by the magnetic fields of the earth. The earth is a big magnetic field with a North and South Pole. When the blood travels through the circulatory system and passes through the lower extremities, it picks up a charge from the electromagnetic fields in the earth that affects the magnetic part of the physical aspect of everyone's personal narrative.

This is important to understand because the magnetic field effects all living organisms which must adapt to control critical cellular systems, such as complex circadian rhythms. Many birds, reptiles, mammals, and fish, even everyone's favorite oddball animal, the duckbill platypus, use electromagnetic fields to navigate and sense prey. For example, birds such as snow geese that migrate over thousands of miles every year have a spot of tissue in their heads which concentrates the mineral, magnetite. In effect, they have a tiny bar magnet built into their brains which they use to navigate from Africa to Siberia over the Himalayas. Ever notice how some people never seem to get lost? Some researchers think that we have a similar magnet in our own brains, but some people are better able to use it than others.

As we move into the emotional aspect, we move from the intangible realm of pure thought and mental images to the semi-tangible world of emotion. An emotional state has real and immediate manifestations-- tears or smiles, happiness, or depression, or it can just make us lie down and fall sleep. Emotion becomes tangible as it moves through the body, pulling on the muscles in our faces, tightening our vocal cords, opening our tear ducts, or pushing out squirts of adrenalin in our bloodstream.

The following patient will demonstrate how her initial thought creates her mental image, which will produce her emotion. Her emotion created chemical responds in her body to maintain her being overweight. The good news is that you will understand why this woman is happy being overweight and had no intentions of losing any weight.

Let's take a look at the interaction of mind and matter. This time, we'll talk about the mysterious phenomenon of spontaneous healing or spontaneous remission. These events involve real pathologies which can be detected in blood tests, imaged, even palpated, so the course of such events has a sharply defined physical reality. Let's review a couple of these mind over matter cases.

Becoming Younger By Thought

In September 1981, a group of eight men in their 70's and 80's, participated in a study in a monastery in Peterborough, New Hampshire. It was a five-day retreat in which they pretended to be 22 years younger. Psychologist Ellen Langer, Ph.D., headed this study from Harvard. What was unique about this study was that the monastery was set up with everything that was popular in 1959. It was a total re-creation including publications from 1959 like the *Saturday Evening Post*, *Life* magazine, and music from Nat King Cole and Perry Como. The men only had discussions about current events from 1959, such as Russian Premier Khrushchev and his relationship to the United States, as well as leaders such as Fidel Castro and his rise to power in Cuba.

Discussions around sports—all the study subjects were men, after all-- involved only the great athletes of that time, such as Mickey Mantle and the boxer Floyd Patterson. By altering their surroundings, the subjects felt that they were living in the 50's. This helped the men imagine that they were twenty-two years younger. What was important in this first group of men is they were constantly thinking of living during 1959, because of the environment and their thoughts and conversations with the other men in the study. For much of the time, their conscious minds were transported back to 1959, even if they did have an occasional thought of 1981. After the five days of the study, the first group of men left, and a second group of men came into the experiment. The second group of men were the control group. They were asked to actively reminisce about being twenty-two years younger, but not to pretend that they were not their current age. At the end of the five days, each group took a battery of tests and vital signs measurements.

At the conclusion of the experiment, all the test findings were compared. One common outcome was that both groups of men were physiologically, functionally, and structurally younger. The major difference was the first group of men who pretended that they were younger, improved more than the control group who only talked about being younger. Other improvements noted were improvements in their height, their gait, and their weight. As their spines straightened, some subjects became taller. Also, as their posture improved, their arthritis appeared to lessen. Touch football became part of their activities. At the end of the five days, some subjects stopped using their pain medications. The ratio of improvement in mental cognition for the first group who pretended that they were living in 1959, was sixty-three percent over the control group which was forty-four percent.

Although both groups enhanced their physical bodies, some subjects altered their body chemistry along with mental changes. They assumed a younger state both physically and mentally. While this was a small study, it was rigorous and the differences in outcomes were statistically significant. The 1959 total immersion treatment acted like the legendary fountain of youth. Mind and matter interacted in a meaningful and positive way.

The next story is an example of how a person who thinks they had surgery-- but did not-- still has a physical improvement. Is that because the thought of a clinical procedure can then produce a mental image leading to an emotion to affect perception enough to alter matter? Let's review the facts and you be the judge.

Feeling Better Without Surgery

In the late 1950's, the *New England Journal of Medicine*, published an article, "An Evaluation of Internal-Mammary-Artery Ligation by a Double-Blind Technique," that assessed a study that compared the then-standard surgical procedure for angina to a placebo surgery where only a small incision was made to have the outward physical appearance of a surgical intervention. To explain, the then standard procedure and technique to address angina was internal mammary ligation, a method that preceded the current coronary artery bypass graft surgery. The procedure was founded on the principle that by blocking damaged arteries, the body would compensate and create new vascular channels to relieve the increased blood pressure. At the time, the surgery generated relief for patients, but physicians could not scientifically prove that the surgery generated new vascular channels. In an experiment, eight patients had their internal mammary arteries ligated, whereas another nine had only superficial incisions to mimic the appearance of the operation.

What happened? Well, five of the eight ligated patients, as well as five of the nine placebo surgery patients, reported significant improvement after the first six months. Interestingly, the study concluded that since the results were the same for both groups, it is possible that the surgical therapy was effective only psychologically and did not improve the physical arteries of the heart. Although the method of internal mammary ligation fell out of fashion as new and improved methods were developed, ligation was popular and helpful for some patients at the time. The study confirmed that both groups, one receiving real heart surgery and the other receiving placebo surgery, reported improved patient outcomes. What does this tell us about the interplay of thought, emotion, and actual well-being? Can a powerful thought do as much as a surgeon's scalpel? In some cases, this not only can happen, but it has also been shown to happen.

5

SUMMARY OF THE THREE ASPECTS (SMOKING EXAMPLE)

Before we enter the last aspect of The Big Four Process, I would like to mention another way of looking at the process of how thoughts, electrical in nature, are the language of the brain, while the emotions are the language of the body, while the physical aspect is magnetic in nature. The Big Four Process is just an organized way of following the body's own inner workings as tiny vibrations become thoughts, emotions, and physical manifestations. The late comic, George Carlin, said that electricity is just organized lightening. Our process takes that small scale lightening that sparks in the brain and makes it useful and accessible, so we can get control of and thus change negative outcomes as they work their way into our physical reality.

The Lab Rats

Each of the case histories we sketched in earlier deals with a different set of particulars—different people with very divergent needs. To make the inner workings of the Big Four Process a little easier to follow, let's take a look at four hypothetical examples of four people, all of whom are trying to do the same thing —quit smoking. We use this example because quitting smoking is exceedingly difficult to do and so many people try so many different approaches to smoking cessation, often with at best partial results. As the old joke says, quitting smoking is easy— I've done it dozens of times.

With that in mind, let's see what happens with our hypothetical lab rats. We will look how each aspect of the Big Four Process, spiritual, mental, emotional, and physical. You will see how each aspect of the Big Four Process will determine if the goal is accomplished or not. With each chapter, it will illustrate the concepts we've just covered.

Scenario: The men wake up one morning and all of them decide that this is the day they will get serious about quitting smoking. For this chapter, we will follow Tom's story. Tom's situation is pretty typical. He's thought seriously about stopping many times, but Tom keeps making the same rookie mistake— Tom complicates and confuses his good intentions with off topic thoughts. He lets his mind wander into recollections of his previous attempts. See if any of Tom's thoughts also rattle around in your head when you approach a challenging task:

- I've tried this so many times before and it's never worked.
- I don't think I have the strength of will say no to another cigarette.
- I'll be so embarrassed if I fail again.
- I just don't think I can do this.

By not acting immediately on his first thought—I stop smoking NOW-- Tom feels he is not fully committed to stop smoking. Tom lights up by late afternoon, says to himself, "What was I thinking? See, I can't do this."

Remember what we said about an idea, a thought as a pure vibration, a little burst of energy deep in our mind. Well, what do you suppose happens when you let those ideas run all over each other the way Tom did? A positive thought is a precious thing, to be nurtured, not confused, or obscured with past doubts and ancient failures. The first part of the Big Four Process is a way of disciplining your thoughts, so they work for you, not against you. Keep that in mind while we move into the next aspect.

Now, let's go back to our lab rats who are trying to stop smoking. Remember that Tom's conscious mind wanted to quit smoking (only 5%), whereas his subconscious mind (95%), kept thinking about what his father said about him not being able to quit. This thought overpowered his ability to move to the second aspect, the mental, because the emotions triggered by his personal narrative were stronger than Tom's desire to quit smoking. For Tom thought became a cul-de-sac he could not escape.

Now let's see what happens with Bob. Bob mastered the thought, but the mental images he developed were based on his false beliefs due to his past experiences. His mental image became fixed on his mom and dad, all the people at work that said he could not quit, and his wife who smoked like the proverbial chimney and had no intentions of quitting. Bob was sabotaged by images embedded in a personal narrative that he could not overcome. Without the process and some expert coaching, he could not overcome the limitations of his experiences.

Let us see now how Randy, our next lab rat, is making out since he is using three aspects—thought, mental, and emotional. Randy is a little more confident that he can stop smoking. One eventful morning, Randy was thinking about all the benefits of not smoking. Randy plans on joining a gym to start working out daily. He plans to tell his friends and family not to smoke or discuss smoking in his presence. He also decided to not take his breaks at work with people who smoke. With this scenario, there is a good chance that Randy will accomplish his wish to stop smoking. What happens? In the next chapter, we will discuss the final aspect of the Big Four Process, the physical, and check in with Randy.

6

PHYSICAL ASPECT OF THE BIG FOUR PROCESS THE BIG FOUR PROCESS

Now, the last aspect, the physical, is the most important because this is the end result-- what you produce in your physical world. This is where that little, almost imperceptible vibration we started with becomes an action, a word, an event, where it impacts your world and potentially those around you. This is the point where thought becomes life, wonderful life.

By now, you might be thinking, "Why did I become the person I am?" In outline, it's simple. The you of this moment is the sum of your past experiences, the things you've done, the people you've met, the places you've been. Everything, whether you consciously remember it, has made an impact, has conditioned your thinking, molded (or warped) your personality, given shape and color to how you see other people.

This is especially true of those key years from birth to age seven, including family experiences, television shows, commercials, what you read, what you heard in church or on a street corner, from friends, from group pressures whether cults or gangs, or just the kids you hung out with on the playground.

The infinite variety of these past experiences is why every person does not react the same, in the same situation.

Now, let's take a look at five real life examples of the physical aspect. Each of the examples demonstrates how the same Big Four Process components have different outcomes based on each unique personal narrative. These examples will demonstrate how your thoughts connect to your personal narrative to answer the question, "Who Am I?" Recall the 95/5 rule we discussed earlier. Your conscious mind, that conversation you have in your head with yourself or even with other people, tells you who you would like to be, who you think you should be--but your actions march to that different drummer in your subconscious mind. You are not always who you think you are. Understanding that other person buried in your personal narrative can be the key to success in any endeavor.

Connecting Consciousness with Science

These first two examples explore the concept of The Big Four Process, in reference to our sense of well-being. As we noted way back in our opening discussion, many individuals will not have an emotional response to the mental image of a tiger, when they know it is not a real breathing, on the back of your neck tiger, and thus it will not affect their physical aspect.

However, if an actual tiger was standing in front of the individual, its hot breath caressing the person's face, the strong scent of feline musk in his nostrils, the situation would be very, very different. The individual would experience a fight or flight impulse, which would take over immediately, resulting in a major alteration of the individual's physical body due to an array of electro-chemical signals, such as increased heart rate and faster breathing, dilated pupils, pale or flushed skin, and trembling muscles.

As a side note, in an article by Kendra Cherry called, "Very Well Mind," she states that being in a constant flight or fight mode has a serious effect on a person's immune system, reducing its effectiveness. This is important because many of my patients feel that they are always under stress in flight mode, and it may be affecting their health long term. With this in mind, let's check our first of five examples.

First Example
Living Longer - A Positive Effect

In the 1930s, a group of young women authored detailed personal essays about their lives. These writings were put aside and forgotten until some sixty years later when three psychologists from the University of Kentucky happened to discover these letters. Deborah Dammer, David Snowdon, and Wallace Friesen, the three psychologists, were conducting research on aging and Alzheimer's disease during that time, and one of them happened upon this collection of essays. They realized that this material could be useful in tracking long term outcomes based on initial circumstances.

They studied the writings and scored the value of each of the personal essays on a scale based on the quantity of positive emotions. There were two unique findings in this study. The first finding was the positive emotions expressed in the writings seem to correlate with this group of women living ten years longer than the typical life expectancy for their population cohort and sociological circumstances. The second finding was that this group of women all became nuns. They concluded that positive thinking leads to living longer-- an important connection to "The Big Four Process."

I call your attention to this study because of a specific finding in the research that the effects of positive emotions can create pathways which can enhance life. As pointed out in the associated research, there are several studies on negative emotions such as anxiety, anger, and sadness. The major reason why studies are focused on negative emotions is because it is easier to identify and study these symptoms, whereas it is difficult to locate and study positive emotions which seem less likely to call attention to themselves.

The article suggests that the increased ten-year life span for the nuns occurred because they were not under stress and not living in a daily "fight or flight" survival mode. Their emotions allowed them to stay in a positive mindset, with harmony in their physical state. This positive outlook was due to the way the nuns processed their life experiences which they based on the Bible. This, in turn, helped to shape their personal narrative. When an individual's body is in "fight or flight" mode, there are several physiological changes in the body, such as increased blood flow to the large muscles of the legs and an increase in focus on survival. A core of negative emotions would hold the individual in this on-the-edge state of survival mode until something shifts to alleviate the fear. The "flight or fight" response effects all systems of the body negatively.

Clearly, a habit of positive thinking has a direct effect on well-being. These women were more concerned about personal growth and solving problems and not in living in survival mode. These findings relate to the first two aspects of The Big Four Process -- emotional and mental and show that the nuns experienced an increase in life span without the kinds of changes in their daily routine, such as physical exercising, dieting, or taking supplements, that so many people resort to today.

The opposite result turns up in our next example which demonstrates how the power of television can alter a generation's old belief system in a very short time.

Example Two
Thought Aspect Shifts the Physical Aspect

This example shows how the first two aspects of The Big Four Process, thought and mental, can create a change in the last two aspects-- emotional and physical, and how an individual's past personal narrative affects their well-being. In 1982, Anne E Becker, an undergraduate student at Radcliffe College, began her research in the Fiji Islands on the eating habits of the Indigenous society. Becker's findings concluded that the eating habits of the Fiji culture were influenced by two external factors; the weather for growing local crops, and the natives' ability to catch fish. Since harvesting a good crop and bringing in fish are both so unpredictable, there were no guarantees of a constant food source to feed the population. This chronic uncertainty created the value system underlying the consumption of food in their culture.

Becker noted that food played a key role in the island traditions within families and communities. Indeed, prosperity was traditionally associated with women having a larger frame, being more robust, and looking well fed. Twenty years later, Dr. Becker, now a Harvard Medical School Psychiatrist and PhD, oversaw another project in Fiji from 1995 to 1998. This study looked at the effects of television in relationship to the cultural norms in Fiji. Television was not a part of the Fiji culture before 1995, so this situation created a natural experiment.

The new research evaluated the effects of television on behaviors related to eating disorders to find out how it was possible for a group of adolescent girls to alter their eating habits in a negative way due to watching television without any signs of physical change or disease. By 1998, just three years after the introduction of television in Fiji, there was a major change in the eating habits of teenage girls due to the images they were exposed to, which included seductive commercials and sexy soaps operas. The Western ideal of beauty and thinness began to be adopted and clashed with the traditional Fiji culture of that time.

Before the introduction of television in Fiji, there were none of the eating disorders which were common in the West. It appeared that eating disorders occurred due to the altering of personal narratives from images seen on television. Being exposed to television for three years resulted in 11.3 percent of adolescent girls reporting that, in order to lose weight, they purged occasionally. In 2007, three hundred girls were interviewed. Findings showed the following:

1) Forty five percent of the girls had purged in the last month.

2) In some cases, girls used appetite stimulants which created a disorder called *macake,* which is a Fijian term meaning a disorder of suppression of the appetite.

3) Twenty five percent of the girls reported thoughts of suicide in the past year.

4) Due to the influence of television, fifteen percent of the girls reported physical attacks from a family member due to their weight loss philosophy.

Clearly a change in ideation, inspired by simply watching television, went on to upset centuries of tradition and overturned basic ideas of female beauty and health. That's a pretty dramatic impact from nothing more than a few ordinary and ephemeral programs and commercials. The same thing happens all the time in our society, but the fact that television was introduced to a traditional society so abruptly made the impact obvious and sudden, not as subtle, and incremental as it has been here at home in the US.

Remember the lemon example were thinking of a lemon caused a change in the physical body? Well, the next two examples demonstrate the dramatic power of thought to reorder our physical world.

Example Three
Worried to Death

Nick Sitzman was married with a wife and two children. He was healthy and ambitious, but he was also known as a notorious worrier. He routinely worried about the worst things that could possibly happen. He was employed by a railroad and worked as part of a crew. On his foreman's birthday, the employees were told that they could leave early. This upset the usually very well-organized operation of the crew.

Sitzman was working in a refrigerated boxcar, and in the confusion, was accidentally locked inside. As Nick tried to open the door, he panicked. He banged the door so much that his fists began to bleed, but his usual crew partner wasn't there. When the crew found Nick next morning, he was dead. He had scratched on the wooden floor with his knife that he was starting to freeze, and he felt like parts of his body were getting numb. The autopsy results showed that Nick had all the signs of extreme hypothermia.

But-- the refrigeration in this boxcar was not functioning at that time and the temperature was fifty-five degrees. Nick altered his physical state by his thoughts. His mistaken thinking that he was in danger in a freezing boxcar caused his death. The power of thought can change the physical body. In this case, thought created a situation where Nick died due to his mistaken perception. Had the refrigeration unit been working properly, he would have frozen, of course. His expectations overrode his physical reality. Yes, friends, your mind can kill you all by itself. A wrong idea is not a harmless error.

Example Four
I'd Rather Die Than Go To Work

Another research study involved two thousand nine hundred and six patients with myocardial infarctions. The time and date of death were recorded for one thousand nine hundred and one of those patients. The most frequent day and time of a heart attack was on Monday, between seven to ten in the morning hours. Could some of these deaths be related to the patient's personal narrative and the work environment? We know that some segment of the population often says they would rather die than go to work. In general, deaths like these heart attacks, and other deaths not due to physical trauma, do not occur randomly across the calendar. They group around certain life events—just before going to work or just after a major holiday. Even when the body is severely impaired, the mind still has a degree of control about when to let go.

Example Five
The Power to Save a Loved One

As we have pointed out several times, the subconscious mind does not know the difference between good or bad, right or wrong, in any moral or philosophical sense. We noted a moment ago, that if someone on a subconscious level would rather die than go to work, then that person will die. But the opposite is also true.

Let's look at a report of teen sisters lifting a 3,000 tractor to free their trapped Dad after a freak yard accident and how this amazing event shows the emotional aspect in physical action. On April 6, 2013, two sisters, Haylee, fourteen, and her sixteen-year-old sister Hannah from Lacomb, Oregon, were approaching their home after a day at school. Upon approaching the house, the sisters heard screaming from the back of the house. When the sisters entered the back yard, they realized that it was their father screaming, "Save me, help me, God." The sisters saw their father pinned under a three-thousand-pound tractor. The tractor had flipped over onto Jeff, thirty-six, who was attempting to remove a stump from the yard.

The girls had "super strength" after seeing their father being crushed and pinned under the tractor, his life being squeezed out of him each time he screamed. The sisters gripped the tractor and lifted it high enough that their father could wriggle his torso free. Events like this are not that unusual. We can find any number of stories, for example, a mother lifting a car off her toddler. But let's ask this-- what would have happened if the sisters came across this same situation, but with a stranger pinned under a tractor instead of their father? We can't really know, of course, but we do know that well documented examples of this kind of super strength usually involve rescuing a loved one, leading us to suspect that it's the emotional connection that triggers the incredible physical reaction.

As we have just seen, there are many ways to demonstrate how the physical can be affected by the emotional, either in a moment of crisis or over a period of time, even a lifetime. In the first example, we saw a positive result-- the nuns in the study lived most of their lives thinking positive thoughts because their environment was positive. In the second example, however, the young girls from Fiji accessed all aspects of The Big Four Process, mental, emotional, physical, and spiritual, which resulted in a negative effect in a handful of years. Television altered thoughts, which affected their mental image of themselves, which then created a negative emotion and unhappy feelings about their physical state, which then altered their body image. The personal narrative can powerfully affect well-being in either a positive or a negative way.

In Nick's case, the frozen railroad worker, his personal narrative created a response in his physical body very quickly—within a night. Whereas, the group of 70-year-olds we looked at earlier, took a full five days. Being in an environment where their thoughts, mental images and emotions allowed them to believe that they were young again, affected their physical body very positively. Their results should remind us of the 911 example, a case of group consciousness on a smaller scale all connected by The Big Four Process.

You will be able to see now how John, our fourth hypothetical lab rat, could quit smoking because John incorporated all four aspects of the Big Four Process: mental, emotional, physical, and spiritual. John had the right thoughts and mental images that made all the difference. John writes a list of all the benefits of not smoking to keep him in the emotional state of not smoking. He then makes a poster highlighting all the benefits from his list and he posts it on his wall. John makes copies of his list of benefits and places copies at work, in his bathroom, and even carries a copy in his wallet. To help the physical aspect John makes an appointment with a hypnotist and a psychologist.

John tells his wife that after he stops smoking, she will be next to follow in his footsteps, multiplying his public commitment. Besides not taking breaks with people that smoke, he also told his friends and family not to smoke or discuss smoking in his presence. John left nothing to chance. He changed his personal narrative in multiple ways simultaneously and nailed the physical reaction he wanted—not smoking. Each link in the Big Four Process chain supported the other links.

In the next chapter, we will summarize and discuss how to use the Big Four Process card deck to help you sort out and mobilize the parts of the process to suit your own personal narrative.

7

SUMMARY OF THE BIG FOUR PROCESS AND THE BIG FOUR PROCESS CARDS

This is where we put it all together! By now you understand that you are four parts being, and that on some level, you can do anything when those four parts are reconciled. You learned about different amazing outcomes, both positive and negative, all depending on the subconscious mind of the person experiencing the event.

There is a saying that everyone has heard one time or another, "Survival of the fittest." If no human interferes with mother nature, what will be, will be. The weakest elk will die by the jaws of the strongest wolf pack because that elk was the slowest in the chase. The baby alligator born with a deformed tail will die because he is now easy prey for other animals—even other alligators. What separates the survival of humans from the survival of the fittest in the animal kingdom? The fact that humans can think, and humans have conscious agency and can direct events, not merely endure. We humans sometimes think that we are smarter than mother nature. But the very strength of our intelligence may become our downfall, our weakness.

Think about it: every human subconscious is constantly being altered by the events it is exposed to, what it is taught in schools or by government, family, religion, what it sees and hears every day in the media, what it is taught by the back and forth of life itself. The web of life we call nature has been here since the dawn of time. Life forms like bacteria, archaea, and fungi go back over four billion years according to science. Humans, us *homo sapiens*, have been around a few hundred thousand years at most. But we think we know more that our conscious mind rules. Our deep subconscious merely laughs and runs the show, while we wonder why our life does not match our conscious desires and intentions.

The Big Four Process can teach you how to discover what your truth is: what's really happening in your subconscious. People all react differently to the same situation, which would not of happen if they were a group of herd animals like deer or zebras. All the animals in the herd would have reacted the same because they all had thoughts that were not altered by the beliefs of other animals.

I see this all the time in my practice. Patients want to change some action in their lives, but do not take the necessary steps to change their personal narrative, because overall, they feel happy with themselves. I refer to that as "they drank the Kool Aid," meaning that they have internalized so many messages from people, commercials, governments, companies, religion—all those actors in their lives that would rather control them instead of supporting their autonomy.

That is why the first part of my message is so simple-- you can change. Although no one person by themselves can change the world, the Big Four Process can change one person at a time, and that is the only way we find happiness or contentment—one person at a time. If you were told, as you were growing up, by your parents, bosses, significant others, etc., that you were unsatisfactory in some form, some way, you now can change that locus of dissatisfaction.

The question I always hear, which you might be thinking right now is, "How do I change when I have been like this my whole life?" To that I say, "It is a choice to change," and for the first time, you can discover and then change the hidden subconscious thoughts preventing you from changing by following the Big Four Process. This is the peeling the onion that I talk about all the time—getting deep down inside your personal narrative to find the dysfunctional beliefs. How do you start a journey of 1,000 miles? One step at a time! Let's start your personal journey now, knowing that "nothing is missing in your life, it is just misplaced in your soul." You already have everything you need, but some deep-seated beliefs are misunderstood, stated incorrectly, linked incorrectly, or even suppressed.

The following is the outline of the Big Four Process, and the description of the card deck.

The first step would be written on a piece of paper what situation you want to start to revise or improve and place it in your pocket, so it is in your energy field. The problem or situation could be about money, relationships decisions, guilt, sickness, etc. It may seem minor or overwhelmingly complex. No matter, it is your starting point.

The following would be an example of what to do with the Big Four Process. For our first exploration, we will use something external and commonplace: "What are my false beliefs about making money?" (See Figure 1).

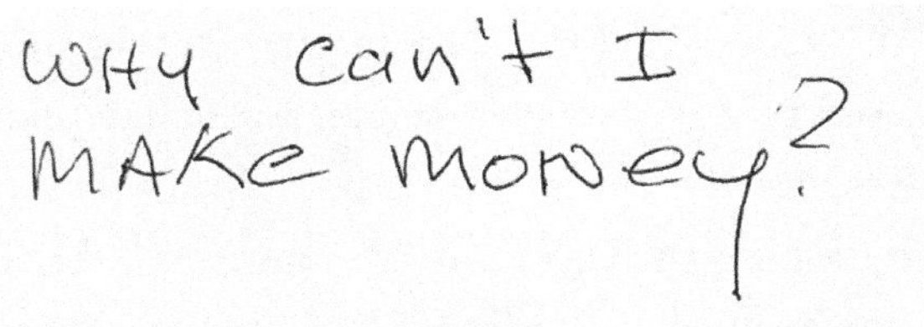

Figure 1: *Write on a piece of paper a question and place it in your energy field.*

A unique factor in the creation of The Big Four Process cards is the development of a connection between the energetic field of the person using the cards and the actual cards themselves. We symbolize this formation through a sacred geometry which is printed on a pendulum and on each of the thirty-six cards. Clip the pendulum over your heart area to connect to the thirty-six cards. This is intended to help you think outside the usual box. Clearly, your usual approach to understanding your issues with money in this example hasn't been working. The cards help you think in a new way without simply turning over the same ideas again and again.

By using the cards, you can refocus and see your situation in a new light. (See Figure 2)

Figure 2: *Picture of the sacred geometry and a sample picture of The Big Four Process cards.*

The Big Four Process card deck contains thirty-six cards. Before we go to step four and using the cards, we will explain each of the cards. Remove the cards and place them in four piles. One pile each containing the seven tan Mental cards, the ten purple Emotional cards, the twelve green Block Energy Points, and the seven yellow Location cards. (See Figure 3)

Figure 3: *The thirty-six cards stacked in four piles.*

Now that you have them set out in neat piles, let's talk first about the seven Mental cards. Each card represents an energy center, the first energy center is *I am*, the second is *I feel*, the third is *I do*, the fourth is *I love*, the fifth is *I speak*, the sixth is *I see*, and the last energy center is *I understand,* the seventh energy center. Each card helps you explore a different important part of your internal energy process—the place where every action begins.

Start your journey in the Big Four Process by first setting up the Big Four Process cards called Mental cards. Each Mental card represents an energy center. On the next page are the Mental cards and what each energy center means. (See Figure 4)

Figure 4: *Mental cards showing meaning of each energy center.*

1. The first energy center, *I am*, is in relationship to the way your family or your situation relates to you (the energy you get from them.)
2. The second energy center, *I feel,* relates to how you see your family or situation (the energy you project towards them.)
3. The third energy center, *I do*, relates to how do you attempt to do something in a situation (are you direct, furtive, do you manipulate or strike out boldly?)
4. The fourth energy center, *I love,* relates to how you love or do not love (maybe hate?) the situation at that time. It may be positive to you, but negative to other people.
5. The fifth energy center, *I speak*, is how you communicate in a situation, are they your words or someone else's?

6. The sixth energy center, *I see,* is how do you see the situation in your eyes.
7. The seventh-energy center is one of the most important ones. *I understand,* it is what I consider the connection to your God. How do you understand the situation through your eyes or through your understanding of divine intent?

Now, that you understand the Big Four Process Mental cards aspect, let's review the meaning of the ten purple Emotional cards. The ten purple Emotional cards are the third aspect of Big Four Process. Remember, when you are going to pick this card, or any Big Four Process cards, it represents the subconscious not the conscious mind. (See Figure 5)

The conscious mind will bend the truth whereas the subconscious mind does not. This Emotional card selection is the third aspect and relates to the Mental card that would have been chosen a moment ago.

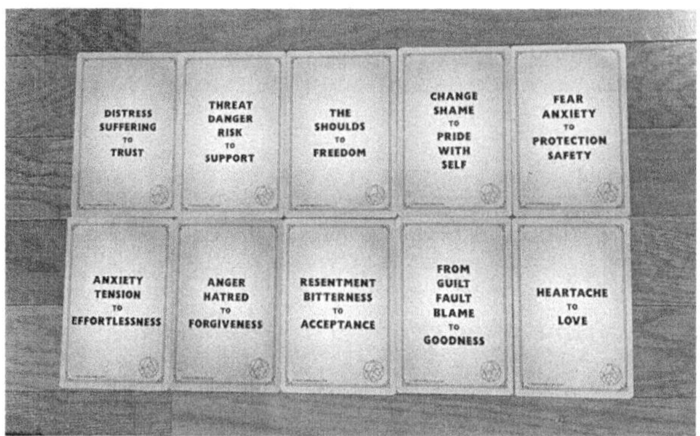

Figure 5: *The ten Emotional cards front and back view.*

Explanation of the ten purple Emotions cards in the Big Four Process:

- The first purple card is changing shame to pride.
- The second purple card is changing anger and hatred to acceptance.
- The third purple card is changing distress and suffering to trust.
- The fourth purple card is changing anxiety and tension to effortlessness.
- The fifth purple card is changing resentments and bitterness to forgiveness.
- The sixth purple card is changing threat, danger, and risk to support.
- The seventh purple card is changing fear and anxiety to protection and safety.
- The eighth purple card is changing heartache to love.
- The ninth purple card is changing guilt, fault, and blame to goodness.
- The tenth purple card is changing obligation to freedom.

Although, there are hundreds of emotions in The Big Four Process, I used the ten emotions that I see repeatedly in my practice. There are only two basic emotions-- love and fear. Fear is the absence of love. Love is the highest emotion, and all other emotions are derivatives of love and fear.

With all the patients I treat now, and have for my past forty plus years, I don't believe that any baby born is born spiritually defective or evil. I believe evil develops as the subconscious of a child grows from birth to seven years old. The only two fears that a baby is born with are loud noises and the fear of falling. Everything else is manufactured, created by their belief systems formed through the experiences of growing up. The subconscious thoughts that are embedded in your mind may have come from others, but now that you are an adult, they are yours and the Big Four Process will help you understand and own them.

The Big Four Process cards are a method to help you get past hearing only the conscious voices, those parts of your personal narrative that try to dominate every conversation inside your head. Your conscious mind is like that overbearing relative you try to avoid—always talking loudly about his opinions and feelings and paying no attention to yours. How do we shut this guy up so we can hear our internal dialogue that tells us who we really are and what we really feel?

Well, here's a simple example, a little trick I learned from a friend who learned it from his grandfather many years ago. You have a simple yes or no decision to make, but everything you do leaves you paralyzed. Yes, seems right, but then so does no. You go back and forth with no conclusion. So, you take a coin from your pocket. Any coin will do. You decide which side, heads, or tails, is yes and which is no. Then you flip the coin.

Here's where you have to be honest with yourself. The moment that the coin lands—heads or tails—you will have an immediate reaction—good or bad. You will be pleased or disappointed in that split second before your conscious mind can process the result. THAT is your true decision. That instant reaction is your authentic inner voice telling you what you really want before any "yes, but" words invade your thoughts. Believe in yourself and follow through with that instant tingle of delight or disappointment and you will be true to yourself. Keep that simple example in mind as we explore how to use the Big Four Process cards to uncover your true inner voice.

8

BLOCK ENERGY POINTS OF THE BIG FOUR PROCESS

Now that the Mental and Emotional cards are explained, let us talk about the Block Energy Points. There are twelve green Block Energy Points, also known as meridians. In the Big Four Process, the twelve meridians cover the whole body for locating the physical aspect of interest in each quest.

Each meridian represents a different organ system. This physical aspect must be expressed in everybody in some way. My favorite saying to explain this to a patient is this: when you take time off by your choice, it is called a vacation, but when God chooses for you, it's called disease. Please remember that other than direct trauma, your physical aspect is the last to be affected. (See Figure 6)

Figure 6: *The Block Energy Points both sides.*

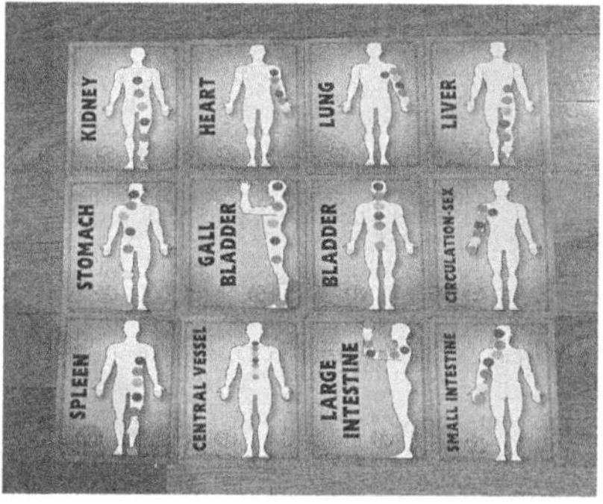

Remember the women who was depressed because she said she had a blood test to prove it? Again, what came first-- the depression or the thoughts of depression? Due to the fact that she was depressed for a certain amount of time, the blood test followed as the experience of depression worked on her bodily systems, possibly affecting the meridians affecting the physical body.

The last set of cards are the seven yellow Location cards. These cards direct your subconscious to the specific organ point in the specific meridian that your subconscious chooses using the green Block Energy Points. For example, if you pick the green Block Energy Points card that has the liver meridian on it, you will notice that there are seven different color circles on it. Each color represents a specific location that the physical block is in the body. Remember, we consist of being four parts, spiritual, mental, emotional, and physical.

The seven Location cards will show where the specific block is in the chosen Block Energy card, along the chosen meridian. (See Figure 7)

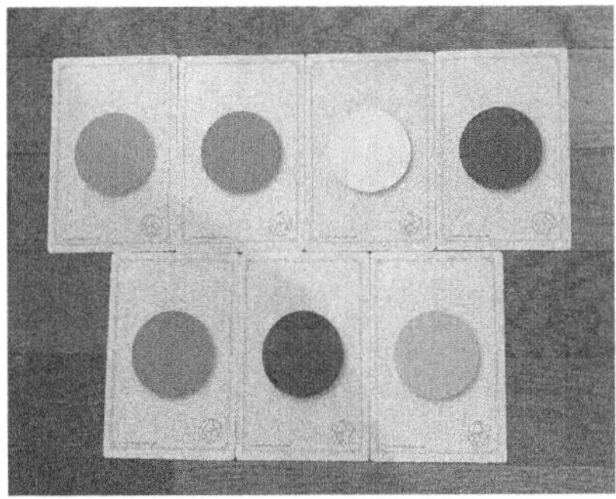

***Figure 7**: The Location cards.*

Each seven yellow Location cards will have one of the seven color circles on it. When the subconscious picks a specific yellow card, it will correlate with one of the color locations on the green Block Energy cards. Each of the seven yellow cards will direct you to one of the specific organ points in each meridian, which you will then include in the Big Four Process meditation, as we will describe shortly. Now that we have reviewed the thirty-six cards and you were introduced to their meaning, let's move on.

The best way to explain the Big Four Process is by an

example from my office. The patient, that we will call Sue, came into my office with a situation about finances. Her subconscious chooses the four cards as seen in the Figure 8. There are over 58,900 different combinations possible.

Figure 8: The four cards chosen by Sue; her truth.

The question that Sue asked was, "Why can't I make money?" By looking at the mental and emotional cards, it appears that Sue was afraid to make money! Sue did not believe that, not realizing that it was her conscious mind talking, not the subconscious mind.

The four cards in Figure 8, chosen by Sue on the mental level, show that Sue has a belief which makes her have a certain feeling, the second energy center **I the FEEL** (the brown card.) The purple card was the **Emotion of SHAME,** which means not being proud to be wealthy. This was what the subconscious mind was stating to Sue which is ninety-five percent of Sue's personal narrative. Sue meanwhile believed on the conscious level that she should be rich.

The reason was that in this case, she excepted her parents' belief system on a subconsciously as truth. It does not matter what Sue's conscious mind thinks, because the subconscious mind will sabotage ever opportunity unless all of Sue's four aspects are connected (spiritual, mental, emotional, and physical.)

When I asked Sue why she would feel shame having wealth, she stated that her parents were poor and had a tough time raising the family as she was growing up. I then asked Sue if she could pull up to her parent's house in a $125,000 automobile, she immediately said, "NO." With this subconscious belief system from her parents, Sue will never be wealthy, no matter how hard she tries.

The green Block Energy card was the small intestine (Figure 8), and the yellow location card was blue, located on the side of Sue's head. This is where the physical block of the Big Four Process occurs. What was also interesting, is that the physical block occurred in the small intestine meridian. In this case, Sue had stomach problems. Due to the laws of thermodynamics, if energy is not expressed **through** the body as **balance emotions,** it will be expressed in the body as **disease.**

Summary of Sue's Situation

Before we explain the fourth and final aspect of the Big Four Process, the spiritual, here is a brief summary of Sue's situation.

Sue was afraid to make money! Sue did not believe that, not realizing that it was her conscious mind talking, not the subconscious mind, which is her truth. Because of her subconscious belief, Sue has the feeling of shame and not pride in being wealthy. In this case, the reason was her parent's belief system that wealth was crass and evil, which Sue subconsciously accepted as truth. It does not matter what Sue's conscious mind thinks, because the subconscious mind will sabotage every opportunity. The physical block in the Big Four Process is the small intestine.

As of now, you have three aspects of the Big Four Process--the mental, emotional, and physical. The spiritual is what we are going to create to connect all four. This is especially important. The key in the Big Four Process is combining all four aspects, spiritual, mental, emotional, and physical, which are all different vibrations together into one vibration. What separates the Big Four Process from other healing arts is that the person knows where the specific physical block is in the body. Going back to the example, Sue understands now that her parents being poor affects the way her subconscious controls her actions. Sue now must shift that meaning of her subconscious belief by connecting the spiritual, mental, emotional, and physical aspects all together at the same time to create a spontaneous change or paradigm shift.

To create this shift, Sue will sit in a chair and feel relaxed--closing her eyes, relaxing, passively listening to soft meditation music like in my office and start thinking the following: Sue will be picturing her parents standing in front her. Her parents are saying in a firm loving voice that it is OK to be wealthy, times were different back then, we need you to be happy, we want you to be happy, we love you, we want you to be successful, we are always with you in spirit, we love you.

Note that it does not make a difference if your parents are alive or have passed on. We are talking here about the memories of Sue's parents as they exist in her subconscious mind, not the day-to-day reality of the nice old folks who still live across town. The key is to feel the emotion, in this case pride. Her parents can be saying to Sue, "You have more opportunities than we ever had." Please remember the more money you make, the happier we are. As Sue hears this from her parents, she will also be repeating many times, "I FEEL PRIDE in Being Wealthy!"

As Sue is stating, "*I feel pride being wealthy,*" she will visualize the right side of her head draining away all the negative thoughts of shame, then becoming clear with pride, filling up her body with pride. As we noted earlier, the spiritual aspect is the process of combining the mental, emotional, and physical aspects of the Big Four Process into a meditation as described above. This process can be done over and over until you feel the new thoughts effortlessly becoming part of how you think.

Asking any question is like peeling the onion back so you can get to the core of who you should be. We have a lifetime of negative thoughts to contend with. Every meditation helps us remove one more increment of the negative thoughts and memories that sabotage us every day. Each mediation is a bite-sized piece of how we get better. Overcoming the drag of a history of negative emotions is a little like eating an elephant—you do it one bite at a time.

Communication With Self
The Last Aspect Of The Big Four Process

The Big Four Process is simply taking one of Sue's beliefs from the subconscious mind to the conscious, so she can recognize it and change it by combining all four aspects spiritual, mental, emotional, physical. Although Sue always wanted to be rich, her conscious mind was always in conflict with her subconscious mind. Sue's subconscious mind couldn't allow wealth to be part of her life because of her parent's situation.

A common question I receive is why the spiritual aspect is

the last aspect to be used as a person is searching for the truth. It is because the spiritual aspect is the highest vibration. I have always believed that this creates the physical aspect in sickness, but in our society, we treat all diseases by the physical aspect first, and usually, only by the physical. Remember the woman who became depressed first and then the blood test changed? The mind and the body are the twins' halves of one event, not separate boxes on a shelf to be taken down one at a time.

Do not get me wrong. If I break my arm, I'll be the first one at the ER. We just need to clarify the difference between emergency care and corrective care. Since I believe that disease is often created by thoughts first, then it does not always make sense to treat the disease from the physical aspect first, we must go back to the source, even as medicine is treating the physical. For example, if smoking causes cancer, yes, we must treat the cancer—surgery, chemotherapy, and any other feasible treatment modality. But, we also must treat the person's need to smoke, to get down to the parts of their personal narrative than drive them to light up and correct that disfunction. All the heroic surgery in modern medicine will avail nothing if we don't stop that need to reach for another cigarette.

We have covered a lot of ideas and actions in this tour of the Big Four Process, but the idea is not really complicated. Everything we've talked about has one goal—helping you get in touch with that subconscious narrative that thwarts your efforts to curb your negative behaviors, that somehow frustrates your drive to get ahead. You know how there are some people we meet that we just can't seem to communicate with? We always talk past one another, even with all the good will in the world.

For most of us, the hardest person of all to communicate with is ourselves. Our conscious and subconscious can't seem to get on the same wavelength. Often, this is even more frustrating because we can't quite see what's going haywire. We just know that we set off to get something done, often to better ourselves, yet we always wind up getting in our own way and failing.

All this talk and our sets of cards and instructions have only one goal—to put you in effective touch with yourself. To let you see the elements in your personal narrative tucked way down in your deepest subconscious that frustrate your best efforts. You see—if you can identify these narrative episodes, you can find the way to overcome them, to develop a meditation, a little mantra all your own, that reminds you and bucks you up when you need it. Sometimes the key to success—any kind of success really, from getting healthier to taking that new job you've been hankering after—is reminding yourself that you are no longer that little child who was ridiculed or hollered at or belittled constantly.

All we are doing with our cards and the Big Four Process is to give you tools to think with, to explore your personal narrative, and identify those terrible but long past painful incidents or difficult words that still haunt you—and banish them. Bad memories, emotional scars draw their power from being dark and hidden. Brought to light, they lose that power. These funny cards can help you shine that light into those corners. That's all this is—a set of tools to help you on your own voyage of self-discovery and healing.

9

PERSONAL PATIENT EXPERIENCES AND THE BIG FOUR PROCESS

In my approach to the Big Four Process, I use the same philosophy employed in Medical Humanities by treating the whole patient: spiritual, mental, emotional, and physical. We don't consider only a part of the patient. For example, if a patient comes in with a rash, treatment is not just about giving the patient a topical ointment or some form of medication, although that may be needed for temporary relief. We look for the underlying cause of the rash as well—an infection? A fungus? A nutritional deficit? With the Big Four Process, there needs to be further investigation of the spiritual, mental, emotional, and physical aspect.

You just learned of the entire process with the example of Sue and her relationship with her parents that influenced her ability to earn a good living and accumulate wealth. The next six examples are additional real life patient stories from my office with many different results. Different results, you ask? Yes. Humans are not made by machines. We all have our quirks and sometimes deep differences in how we see and react to our world. Even a well-known medicine like penicillin doesn't work for everyone. We'll talk about a case soon when the Big Four Process sort of failed. Did it really fail? Read below and you be the judge.

Patient One
Can You Choose Being Overweight Over Love?
A Twenty-Six-Year-Old Female and a Hershey Bar

In my practice, I have experienced that The Big Four Process has a positive effect with my patients' well-being. With this patient, an initial idea of love was misguided, but with the Big Four Process, this patient altered a core belief system relating to her weight. Let's see how this played out.

Patient History: An overweight 26-year-old female came to my office with complaints of indigestion, constant hunger, stress, and depression. She complained of digestion problems and craving fats in the form of peanut butter and cheese. She also said she needed to eat a Hershey bar every day.

While there are many aspects to this patient's personal narrative, for this example, I will focus only on her key statement that she "Needed to eat a Hershey bar every day." This statement is particularly important for exploration using the Big Four Process. Why would this patient need to eat a Hershey bar every day, and what did the Hershey bar represent to her? Clearly it had to be important, more than just chocolate.

After a few visits, we started to break down this patient's false belief system using the Big Four Process. While she was a little girl, every day her grandfather would walk her to the bus stop. Upon her entering the school bus, her grandfather would hand her a Hershey bar.

This Hershey bar became the connection between this patient and her grandfather later in her life. This connection became part of this patient's personal narrative which affected her well-being throughout her life. We discovered that this patient's love connection to her grandfather was transferred to the Hershey bar after he died. The following are the Big Four Process cards that this patient picked subconsciously:

- Mental card was I Love, the fourth energy center
- Emotional card was Heartache to Love
- Block Energy Point card was Liver
- Location card was Blue

After her grandfather's death, when she would think of a Hershey bar, it produced the feeling of love for her grandfather and her personal narrative changed drastically. Since her grandfather was no longer present in her physical life, she altered her Big Four Process by eating a Hershey bar every day. This was her way of maintaining and justifying a connection between herself and her love for her grandfather.

Her love effectively overpowered the last aspects of the Big Four Process, the physical aspect, because she was overweight and could not change it. It did not matter that it was a negative physical response which resulted in her being overweight. The subconscious mind (95%) overrides the conscious mind (5%). She chose to eat the Hersey bar every day because her love for her grandfather was more important to her than love she had for herself. We all know the old saying that food is love, but in this case, it took an odd twist and became a turning point in this young woman's life.

This patient had impressive results after working with The Big Four Process because she altered a core belief by combining the mental, emotional, physical, and spiritual into one paradigm shift. The shift was accomplished by first knowing the four aspects and altering her subconscious. She did not have to actually eat a Hershey bar to remember her love for her grandfather and to honor him. Seems simple, but this Hershey bar is the kind of trick our subconscious can play on us—until we get inside our own heads and understand ourselves. That's the point of the Big Four Process. We struggle to change *what* we do until we understand *why* we do it.

The next patient was also heavy, but although she did not lose weight, with the understanding of the Big Four Process, she is now happy being overweight and feels great about it—another kind of victory.

Patient Two
Father Does Not Love Me
A Forty-Six-Year-Old Female and Her Father

This forty-six-year-old female was severely overweight when she became my patient. Like the prior example, this case also involved the subconscious mind and the connection to a loved one. In this case, the loved one was her father.

This patient chose to be overweight to prove her love to her father. While learning the history of this patient, I discovered the following. While growing up, this patient lived with her parents who had an unhappy marriage. Her father did not pay attention to or spend time with his wife or his children.

She explained to me that she always wanted her father to take time with her. He would not spend weekends at home. No one from his immediate family knew his location or what he was doing on these weekends.

Long after her father died, this patient said that no matter what diet she went on, she could never lose weight. She found herself sneaking food at night when no one was watching her. As always, the history of the patient is especially important.

During one visit we discovered, the connection to this patient's personal narrative, "The Big Four Process," in relationship to her well-being.

When I explored her history, this patient mentioned that every time she would open the refrigerator door, her father would say, "You are going to get fat." Further investigation into that statement showed that there was a personal narrative connection between her father, the refrigerator, and with being overweight. The following are the cards that she chose:

- Mental card was I Feel, the second energy center
- Emotional card was Heartache to Love
- Block Energy Point card was Liver
- Location card was Green

The Big Four Process cards revealed that this patient would do anything for her father's love. This endured as she was growing up and to her surprise, it was still true in her subconscious mind as an adult. Throughout her life, she was always starving for her father's love and attention.

I chose this patient's case history because it is a perfect example to demonstrate the following. The subconscious does not look at positive or negative results. In many situations, it will just do what it was taught as a child, continuing the individual's processing of their subconscious experience, all their imprints, and their experiences in their environment, as they were growing up.

In this case, when her father told this patient that she was going to get fat growing up, her subconscious absorbed it, without a positive or negative judgment. Even as an adult, she still wanted on a subconscious level to receive her father's love, and it was more important to stay overweight than to call her dead father a liar and be skinny to prove him wrong. Irrelevant to the outcome that her father might have intended for this little girl, she subconsciously understood it as he always wanted her to be fat.

Bear in mind that children are not versed in logic. She understood her father's sarcasm as an expression of concern and a rare positive connection between them. An unloved child will grasp at straws, take any possible indication of love, however faint, and cherish it deep in the subconscious. Using the Big Four Process allowed us to uncover this long buried, but still powerful connection to the man who meant so much and gave so little.

The next patient had a different outcome yet again.

Patient Three
My Ego Killed Me

One of my patients had throat cancer. He was in his late fifties when I first met him. At the time, he was the father of two small children from a much younger wife. He was under the medical care of an oncologist and was looking for holistic and nutritional support to add to his therapy.

With the Big Four Process, the history of someone's life is vitally important. During my initial client intake with him, he mentioned that he also had children from his previous marriage. In further discussion, this patient revealed that he had not spoken to his children from the first marriage for over ten years.

This is where the medical humanities approach focusing on the whole patient is so important. He stated that his oncologist focused on the physical aspect of his healing with little concern whether any with other aspects of his life, such as not speaking to his children for years, might have impact on his well-being.

After working with this patient, the Big Four Process cards revealed the following:

- Mental card was I Speak, the fifth energy center
- Emotional card aspect was of Guilt
- Block Energy Point card was Heart
- Location card was Red

With a further history from this patient, we discovered that his children from his first marriage were terribly angry with him because he left their mother for a trophy wife. This situation was further complicated by this patient having a child with his new wife. When I asked this patient when he last spoke to his older children, he responded, “Not for ten years.”

The conflict is first who is not speaking to whom? Do the children from the previous marriage refuse to speak to him or does this patient refuse to speak to them? Also, it appeared from the Big Four Process cards that this patient feels guilty on some level.

We know that energy is neither created or destroyed and can only be transferred from one form to another. Therefore, if the energy of an emotion is not expressed through the body as that specific emotion, it can only be expressed in the body as disease.

An important question that I asked him was, “Did you reach out to your children?” He immediately said, “No,” because they were mad at him. Aha-- that is where the conflict sits.

I tell my patients in this type of situation to “Put the ball in their (the other person’s) court.” There are only two scenarios: Either the children will not speak to their father, or the father will not speak to his children. The best way to make it quite clear to the children that you want to speak to them as their father is to take the action step to contact and tell them that he would love to speak to them and that he was always available for them.

To my surprise, this patient refused to contact his children. I therefore had to release this patient from care after three visits because he was not willing to take steps to shift his energy field.

In this situation, the Big Four Process would not work because this patient refused to alter his emotional aspect. By his refusal to talk to the children, there could be no change in his thoughts. The mental images will not shift, so the same mental image will continue to produce the same emotion, thus continuing the same energy pattern which his body expressed as cancer.

Are you in this category? The Big Four Process will not work if you will not be open. Ask yourself if this were you, and you were in that situation, what would you do? If you had a serious disease would your ego win? If you were estranged from your children for years and it was causing you to be sick, what would you do? The Big Four Process can help you with any number of difficult life situations, but it cannot save you from yourself if you will not make the effort. Talking to his children after ten years of a strained silence would have been certainly painful, but sometimes the Big Four Process takes us to a place where we have to face pain to move beyond it.

Patient Four
Death By Stealing

Everyone's Big Four Process will determine how each situation will affect the person's well-being. That thought is influenced by two things: the landscape, meaning the environment surrounding you, and how the individual processes the landscape.

This next patient, a thirty-six-year-old male patient with brain cancer, became a close friend of mine. He was a good man and had a successful business. What I learned from talking to him and exploring his history was that when he was younger, he took advantage of where he worked. This included using his boss's equipment and inventory and then pocketing the money.

During the telling of his history, he asked, "Do you think I got cancer because of all the bad things I did?" He also said to me, "Do you think I am being punished by God because of my past?" What is difficult here is that he really believed that he was being punished for his wrongdoing. The Big Four Process cards that his subconscious picked were:

- Mental card was I Feel, the second energy center
- Emotional card was Guilt
- Block Energy Point was Central Vessel
- Location card was Blue

The sad news is that this patient passed away very quickly because of how far the cancer had progressed. There was not enough time to address his belief system of being punished due to his actions. More time was needed to alter that belief, which could have altered his well-being during his last days.

Although, there must have been other issues that caused his brain cancer, I personally believe that the thought that God was punishing him played a major part in his early death. If only he had come to me earlier. The Big Four Process does not cure brain cancer, but helping him to a better understanding of his life and a reconciliation with his past, might well have made the final stages of his battle easier. The mere fact that, although seriously ill, he started the process eagerly spoke volumes about his quest for peace of mind. That we all will leave this life is ultimately out of our hands, but how we leave it, beset by turmoil or wrapped in tranquility, that we can control.

Patient Five
How Your Surroundings Change with Five Children

Being in practice for over 40 years, I have watched families grow and I have treated three generations of the same family. I have had the pleasure of seeing families grow from one child to many children. I have witnessed the success and happiness of some families, while I saw sadness consume others.

The patient I want to mention here is part of a family that I treated; husband, wife, and their three children. What was interesting to me about this family is that I treated the wife when she was a child, and then years later, I also had her three children as patients. This patient was 24 years old when she had her first child, twenty-nine years old when she had her second, and thirty-nine years old when she had her third child.

I noticed that this twenty-four-year-old mother did not treat her baby the same as when she was a twenty-nine-year-old mother, and even more differently when she was thirty-nine. All parents change as their family grows and time passes, but in this case, my patient's circumstances were completely different. After the birth of her second child, this patient became extremely sick, so by the time she had her third child, her health was seriously impaired.

All three children experienced a different mother. The first child had a completely different childhood than her younger siblings. The second child experienced a mother who became sick in her younger years and then slipped into a long decline. The third child was raised by an extremely sick mother from the time she was born to her teenage years and felt the full effect of her mother's sickness in her own personal narrative. She experienced "The Big Four Process" differently than her other two siblings who were raised by a mom who was healthy and outgoing during their younger years.

This third child was always complaining of some aliment and was always seeking attention, whereas her older siblings did not seek the same attention. In doing the Big Four Process with her, we discovered the following when she chose the cards:

- Mental card was I Feel, the second energy center
- Emotional card was Fear
- Block Energy Point card was Heart
- Location card was Blue

This third child told me during the history that she was afraid that she would become sick like her mother. During her brain pattern development, when her subconscious formed its key concepts, she perceived things differently than her older siblings who grew up with a healthy mother. She would be afraid to come home from school because she did not know in what state she would find her mother. Sometimes her mother would be extremely sick, while other times, as she put it, "Just surviving." She said that her older siblings did not worry as much as she did. They had completed so much more of their personal narratives before they had to deal with their mother's constant debilities.

Children instinctively look to their parents for strength and for models of how adults manage their world. A chronically ill parent inverts normal expectations and causes the child to develop a personal narrative haunted by doubts, dark thoughts, and fears of imminent catastrophe. Alleviating such a narrative is a tall order, but the Big Four Process helped this woman find a way into her abnormal thinking, so that she could face her fears clearly and develop new concepts to replace them.

Patient Six
I Have Resentment and Bitterness Towards You: Does Breast Cancer Have Benefits?

The last patient in my examples is a 58-year-old woman that came to my office with breast cancer. As always, the history is the most important aspect of a patient's well-being. I asked her if there were any dramatic events that occurred in the past year or so before the diagnosis. Her response was that her husband wanted to move to Florida, and she did not want to go. She explained that the relationship between her and her husband was always a little rocky.

The major reason she did not want to go to Florida was because of her grandchildren, whereas her husband was less interested in being involved in the grandchildren's lives. As we went further into her history, I asked her a simple question, "What is the benefit of having breast cancer?" Her response was simply, "There is no benefit." But she was mistaken, there is always a benefit. What this patient realized after the Big Four Process was that by her getting breast cancer, her husband now would not move to Florida. The following cards came up with the Big Four Process.

- Mental card was I Feel, second energy center
- Emotional card was Resentment and Bitterness to Acceptance
- Block Energy Point card was the Heart
- Location card was Green

After doing the Big Four Process by combining all four vibrations with a meditation, this patient had a major shift. She told me that she realized that she may have gotten the breast cancer because she did not want to go to Florida. Instead of facing her husband and telling him that she did not want to go, her love for him turned into resentment and bitterness. Since this patient's resentment and bitterness were not expressed in the body as an emotion, they were expressed in the body as a disease.

This patient did not want to move to Florida, and because her husband would not listen to her or understand what she was saying, so she found another way. Remember, your subconscious does not know the difference between positive and negative thoughts, it just does what takes you towards your goal. In this case, she did not want to go to Florida under any circumstances. This patient's subconscious, the ninety-five percent, answered her command and created her illness to stay in New Jersey.

I have been asked many times what the difference is between forgiveness and acceptance of a person? In the Big Four Process, forgiveness is called for when the emotional card of anger and hatred is chosen by the subconscious mind. Whereas acceptance is used when the resentment and bitterness emotional card is chosen.

The above patient's case is a perfect example of the difference between acceptance and forgiveness. This patient's subconscious chooses the emotional card, resentment and bitterness to acceptance.

My many patients have taught me that when you love someone, you accept that person's action because of what they did. Whereas, when you do not love someone, you forgive them for *who* they are and what they did.

10

WHERE DO I GO FROM HERE?

Where do you go from here? Now that I have shared with you examples of the Big Four Process, it is now your turn to start your journey. A journey of 1,000 miles starts with a first step. If you are reading this information, then you have a running start. You are different, not part of the majority. There is a leader in you, although you may not believe it yet. I am proud of you, for taking a next step by trusting me in your journey.

1) Start by identifying **three** issues in your life-- things you really want to change. All change must start with something real. Nothing changes in theory. For example, here are some of the issues patients have experienced. Are any of these on your list as well?

- Money-- Need more? Need to manage it better?
- Getting in shape-- Need to lose weight?
- Getting healthier?

- Family issues-- How to improve interfamily relationships?
- Work problems-- How to perform better or get along better at work?
- Career-- Need to get your career on track? Where do you go from here?
- Relationships-- Need to deal with all kinds of people better?
- Controlling your emotions? A problem with anger?
- Romantic relationships-- Need to deal with finding/keeping a partner?

2) Next, you need to purchase the Big Four Process cards and pick **one** of the three issues that you identified. You will come back to the others later. Your first-time goal in using the Big Four Process should be challenging, but not too hard. Before using the Big Four Process, try to define the problem as carefully as you can and set the goal(s) you want to achieve. You can't find success unless you know what success looks like. How big is it? What will it feel like? What will you be able to do that eludes you now?

3) Print out the worksheet from the website: Findyourblocks.com. The worksheet that is referenced on the next page. Make sure you make the time and find the place to concentrate while completing the worksheet. You must focus on the Big Four Process. Set aside an hour, which is more than enough for the first time with no kids, no spouse, no interruptions. Set your phone on silent. This is your time for your benefit. Hint-- you're worth it. That's why we're doing this.

Step by Step Using the Big Four Process Cards

Step One: Write on a piece of paper what situation you want to start to clear and place it in your pocket, so it is in your energy field. The problem or situation could be about money, relationship decisions, guilt, sickness, etc. Choose your first question and write it on a piece of paper.

Step Two: A unique factor in the creation of The Big Four Process cards is the development of a connection of the energetic field of the person using the cards to the actual cards themselves. This was accomplished by the formation of a sacred geometry which is printed on a pendulum and each of the thirty-six cards. Clip the pendulum over your heart area to connect to the thirty-six cards.

Step Three: Remove the cards and place them in four different piles by the color of the cards. The Big Four Process card deck contains thirty-six cards. Containing seven tan Mental cards, ten purple Emotional cards, twelve green Block Energy Points, and seven yellow Location cards.

Step Four: You now will start the Big Four Process. Place the seven Mental cards face down in any configuration you choose. You can place them in a straight line or whatever. It is important that they are face down in no specific order.

Step Five: With the Mental cards face down, look at each of the cards and choose the card that feels right for you to select. Your subconscious mind will choose the right Mental card that is in relationship the question in your energy field. Do not look at the card and place it to the side face down.

Step Six; Now place the ten cards labeled Emotional on the table, as you did with the Mental cards. Look at each of the cards that are face down and choose the card that feels right for you. As before, your subconscious mind will choose the right Emotional card that is in relationship to the question in your energy field. Do not look at the card and place it to the side face down with the Mental card that you previously chose.

Step Seven: You now have discovered the mental and emotional aspects of the Big Four Process; you are fifty percent there. It is time to find the third aspect of the Big Four Process. The next two steps will tell you which system in the body is being affected and the specific location of the energy block in your body, the physical aspect of the Big Four Process. Place the twelve cards labeled Block Energy Points on the table face down. As before, your subconscious mind will choose the right Block Energy Points that is in relationship to the question in your energy field. Do not look at the card and place it to the side face down with the Mental card and Emotional card.

Step Eight: After choosing one of the twelve possible Block Energy Points, the next step is to find the specific location of the blocked energy. You now need to find the location on the Meridian in which the block is occurring. This is accomplished by placing the seven yellow Location cards, in any configuration, face down on the table.

Step Nine: At this point, you have chosen the all the cards which represents the disharmony between the question you are holding and your truth. These four cards represent the mental, emotional, and physical aspects of your being which create the final aspect of the Big Four Process.

Step Ten: Turn the four cards (Mental, Emotional, Block Energy Point, Location) over and place them in front of you. To analyze the Big Four cards chosen, you now will develop the last aspect of the Big Four Process, the spiritual. The next few steps will complete the Big Four Process by connecting and blending the four aspects of your spiritual, mental, emotional, and physical into a new understanding and meaning of the question asked.

Step Eleven: Up to this point, you have the three aspects of the Big Four Process. the mental, emotional, and physical. The spiritual aspect is what we are going to create in this process to connect all four aspects into one new thought.

It is important that you know how to do the Big Four Process the right way. When a patient tells me that, "Practice makes perfect," that is not true because only perfect practice makes perfect. If a person practices a gulf swing two hours a day what does that mean? If the person practices the swing wrong for two hours, the result is a waste of time, both for the individual and the gulf club.

Only perfect practice makes perfect, Therefore, to ensure that there is a perfect understanding of the Big Four Process, the following pages will have examples of the Big Four Process. The examples will demonstrate the Big Four Process in different ways. There will be both simple and complex examples, all from my personal patients. It is important to remember that all of the Big Four Process cards were chosen from the patient's subconscious mind, the truth, not their conscious mind.

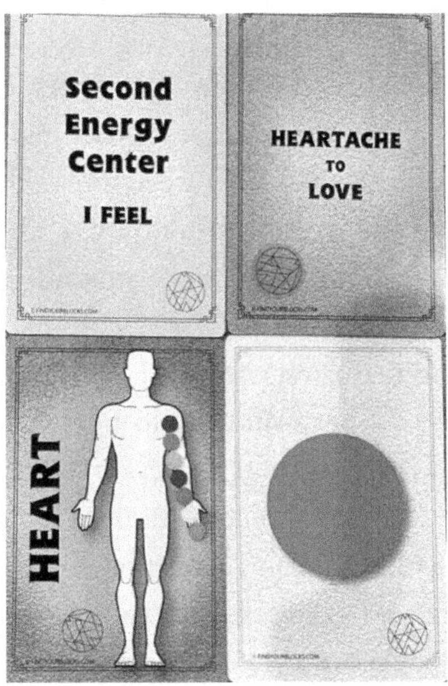

Example One: This patient, Karen, had a situation with love. The question that she held in her energy field was, "Why do I not feel Love?" In this situation, the Big Four Process cards that were drawn related to love. The Mental card was I feel; the Emotional card was heartache; and the Block Energy Point was heart. The Location card was red and is located on the left arm as shown in the pictures.

If you were to pull these four cards, I would ask you the same question I asked Karen. Before, I tell you the question, you need to know this about yourself and everybody else. When a question is asked of you, your first thought is your truth. The answer that is the truth will occur withing three seconds or less. It is important that you do not think but say the first thought that comes to your mind. When a person takes time to think, then the conscious mind is answering the question. It could then be a lie.

The question that I asked Karen was, "What is your biggest heartache in your life?" Within a second, she said "Mom." At this point, I now have enough information, to perform the Big Four Process.

Karen now will use the spiritual aspect of the Big Four Process to connect the other three vibrations of the Big Four Process. The spiritual aspect will be accomplished in the form of a meditation were the mental, emotional, and physical will be combined into one vibration to create a paradigm shift in Karen to alter the subconscious.

What Karen did during the Big Four Process was sit in a chair in meditation. She would say to herself the following, "I feel because that is the mental aspect, love because that is the emotional aspect." She will picture the red location in her arm as the physical aspect as shown on the Physical and Location cards that she chose. During the meditation, as she is saying, "I feel the love that my mom gave me because she did her best with what she had experienced in her life." As she is saying that Karen will visualize the emotion of heartache draining out of her body from the red location point and being replaced with love as she starts the Big Four Process.

Since, Karen's mom was the person she mentioned in reference to the Emotional card heartache, this means that the mom caused her heartache. There are two vital facts that must be mentioned here. First, it does not matter if her mom is alive or has passed, her mom will still have the same negative effect on Karen. Second point is that the subconscious mind chooses the cards, the ninety-five percent, not the five precent conscious mind. The meditation connects the heart to the mind. Karen said that she did not think it was her mother causing her problem when it was, because that was the conscious mind.

The process starts by Karen sitting in the chair listening to relaxing music. She started the connection of the heart and mind by saying, "I feel the love that mom gave me because, she did her best with what she had experienced in her life." Karen will keep repeating this saying by saying it over and over. It is important that the person doing the Big Four Process feels the positive emotion that is listed on the Emotional cards. In this case, Karen must feel the love for her mom.

Sometimes a patient states that they feel no love for the person they are trying to clear. This occurred in the case of Karen's mom. What I would say then is the following. "Karen did you ever love a pet or anything?" If yes, then transfer that feeling to her mom. Karen must feel the emotion of love during the meditation to connect to the vibration.

Summary of Karen's experience. When she combined all for aspects of the Big Four Process, spiritual, mental, emotional, and physical, she shifted her conscious mind to connect with the subconscious to alter a core belief. She is doing this by connecting her heart to her mind. Karen cried as she did the Big Four Process, which in my eyes means we touched her soul.

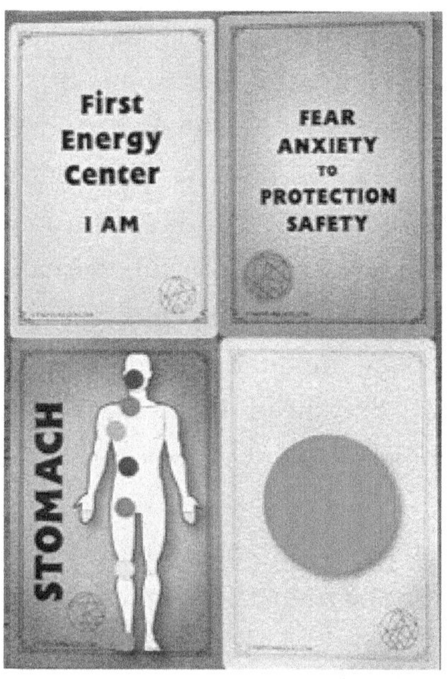

Example Two: Tom enters the office with the following situation. He did not trust anyone which was affecting his whole life including relationships, and his workplace. The question placed in John's energy field was, "Why do I not trust life?" The four cards that Tom subconscious choose was the following. The Mental card was I AM, the Emotional card was fear and anxiety. The Block Energy Point was stomach, and the Location card blue - the bottom of the right foot.

As in the prior example, I asked Tom, "What is the first thing that comes to your mind when I ask you the following question? "What do you fear the most in life?" He said dying. When I asked Tom why, he told me the following story.

He said that when he was young, one night he begged his parents to take him to a local mall to buy a game that he wanted.

It was snowing that night and his parents did not want to go, but he insisted. Unfortunately, on the way home from the store, they were in an automobile accident. Both of Tom's parents were killed, but he was not hurt.

This was a difficult clearing and involved several sessions, but it was not impossible. The vibrations of emotions enter through our feet, and this is where Tom had an emotional block. In the meditation to connect all the four vibrations into one vibration, to produce the heart mind connection, Tom did the following. He would picture his mom and dad saying to him, "You are protected and safe, and we are always here with you to protect you." As he visualizes that his parents are saying this to him, he is saying, "I am safe and protected," the mental and the emotional aspect.

Tom's parents also say to Tom, "We would not have changed anything, we would do it all over again, because we love you that much." As Tom repeats, "I am safe and protected," he pictures fear and anxiety leaving his feet, and protection and safety filling his body. Remember, you must feel the protection and safety.

When I asked Tom when he felt safe and protected in his life, he said something unique. When he was in the womb. That is the feeling that Tom had to have while doing the Big Four Process. Although it took many sessions, Tom did create the heart mind connection because Jo did not give up in his journey.

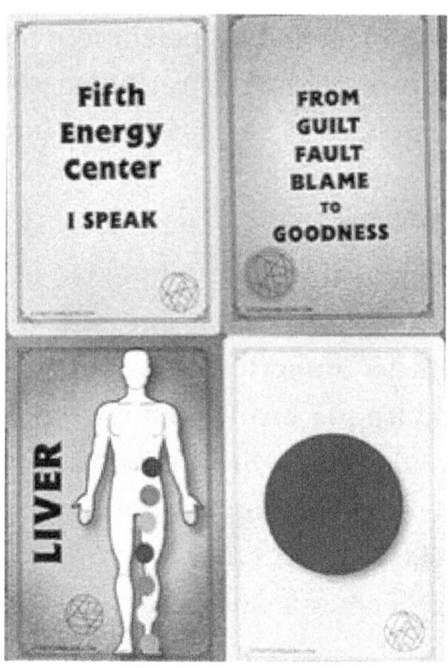

Example Three: John had a situation that was typical of many people, "Not happy." The Big Four Process cards that the subconscious chose were the following: The Mental card was I speak, and the Emotional card was guilt, fault, and blame to goodness. What was interesting was that John was overweight and had extremely high cholesterol. The Block Energy Point was the liver, and the Location card was blue. It was interesting that the liver meridian was affected as physical because of the high cholesterol.

John's major complaint was that he felt guilt, even when he thought he was happy. I always ask that magical question. I stressed to John, "When I ask you this question do not think, I want the first answer that comes to your mind." That is your subconscious mind, the truth speaking, not your conscious mind, your dreams.

If John takes more then 2 -3 seconds, he is lying to himself. Humans are the only species that can justify anything, in some cases, even murder. This is the question that I asked John, "Who is the one person that makes you feel guilty?" and without missing a beat John said "mom."

John's story was that his mother was sick and always wanted him home growing up. Even though she has passed away many years ago, John still has this feeling of guilt. It was funny because in this case, John is Italian, like me, and I said to him, "We had the best teachers in the category of guilt." Since it was the fifth energy center, I speak, I know that John did not speak up to his mother growing up or did not speak his truth.

John speaks to his mother in the mediation of the Big Four Process, "Mom, I want to thank you for doing your best, and I was grateful, and now I can appreciate goodness." As John speaks to his mother, he visualizes his mother is saying to him, "I had to teach you the hard way, because you didn't listen to the easy way. Thank you for learning my son, I love you." As John is saying and hearing this, he is feeling the guilt, fault, and blame energy draining out of his side, as shown on the Location card, replacing it with goodness.

Summary: John did say he was reckless growing up and maybe by his mother being sick, she saved his life. If he was not home taking care of her, he said he probably would be in the streets. With the fourth aspect of spiritual, John was able to create a paradigm shift in his subconscious by connecting all four vibrations simultaneously.

Example Four: Kate was a married woman who was unhappy. She was not quite sure why this feeling of unhappiness was upon her. The question that was placed in her energy field was, "What is happiness to you?" The cards that Kate's subconscious, the truth, pulled was the Mental card I do, which is the third energy center. The Emotional card was the shoulds to freedom. The Block Energy Point card was circulation and sex, with the Location card color brown.

As always, I tell the patient, "I'm going to ask you a question and do not think. I want the first thought that comes to your mind." As mentioned before, the question was, "What is happiness to you?" This is a clearing that has various levels, like peeling an onion back. Her answer was fascinating, as you will soon learn why. It was, "Not being married." What she was saying on a subconscious level that she wishes that she wasn't married. In Kate's case, the Mental card pulled represents self-esteem, so that was part of it.

I asked her again, "If you were not married, what does that mean to you?" The word freedom came up. When the word freedom came up, I told Kate that there are many married women who still have freedom. The next question to Kate was, "What does the freedom represent to you?" With this question, the truth came out. She never followed her dreams.

The Big Four Process cards were unique in this situation because they revealed a deep finding within the subconscious thinking. The meditation that Kate did was that she was standing on a pedestal telling the world, "I now do what I need to do for Kate. I am free to be myself, whatever it takes...going back to school, working, whatever." As Kate is standing on the pedestal repeating that she is visualizing all the "shoulds" in her life, such as I should have done this (like go to school, etc.), all the "shoulds" are dissolving and leaving the Block Energy Point on her right arm and being replaced with freedom.

After the Big Four Process, Kate realized her issue wasn't freedom in her marriage as she thought. She realized it was freedom within herself that was missing in her life and that she needed to develop within her own self-esteem and not from her marriage.

The third energy center, I do, represents self-esteem and what Kate was doing was blaming the marriage for not having any self-esteem. After this clearing, her marriage improved because in this case, her husband worked with her to help her find freedom within herself through self-esteem.

Summary: When you start doing the Big Four Process, start with something simple. In this case of peeling back the onion, Kate had a clear understanding of what she needed to do now to help herself. She understood that she was blaming the marriage when she should have been changing herself. Kate's success in marriage would depend on the family dynamics. At this point, Kate now knows on a subconscious level that she needs to take care of herself. By combining the four vibrations into one vibration, Kate changed her internal belief, and became aware that she could increase her self-esteem or be happy in any situation.

Example Five: In my practice, sometimes patients had a paradigm shift very quickly to a solve a situation. This was the case with Jack. I was treating Jack for nutritional counseling because he was allergic to cheese. It was not a severe allergic reaction, but a mild skin reaction.

During the history I asked him, "When did you became allergic to cheese?" He answered that it started when he was a child. After further investigation, Jack said that he remembers eating cheese one day and his father coming into the kitchen and telling his mother, "Jack will be allergic to cheese, just like me." What is a plus here with the Big Four Process is that since

Jack remembers that statement, it means that it has an effect on him in some way.

In doing the Big Four Process, the question that was placed in Jack's energy field was, "Why am I allergic to cheese?" The Mental card chosen was I AM, which is the first energy center, the family. The Emotional card was anger and hatred to forgiveness, and the Physical card was large intestine, and the Location card was red.

After reviewing the Big Four Process cards chosen by Jack's subconscious, it is important to learn who he is angry with. When I asked Jack, who he was angry with, without thinking and without hesitation, he said "dad." What Jack must do is to connect the mind to the heart by Jack forgiving his father. There had to be some connection to the allergy and his father.

In doing the Big Four Process in the mediation, Jack was telling his father that, "I have forgiveness for you dad because I know you were only trying to protect me." As Jack is saying this his father, Jack is visualizing that his father is saying, "The only reason why I said that was because I love you and did not want you to get sick. "When Jack is saying the mantra, "I have forgiveness for you dad, because I know you were only trying to protect me." He visualizes anger and hatred leaving the Block Energy Point draining and being replaced with forgiveness.

The meditation is the spiritual part that pulls all of the other three aspects together, connecting of all four vibrations to create a new core belief. A few months after this clearing, Jack was completely allergy free from cheese.

Go through the Big Four Process one step at a time. Don't hurry, be deliberate. No prizes for speed. Have all the materials set out in front of you. After you complete your first clearing of the subconscious connection to the conscious mind, you will be amazed at the results.

The Big Four Process is a learning experience that adds to

previous experiences. It is like reading a book. The second time you read the same book, you will have a different perception from the first time because you are not the same person that you were when you read it the first time. The only constant in the universe is change, therefore, each time you complete the Big Four Process, you will become more enlightened in your life.

I have been asked, "Are there any drawbacks to the Big Four Process?" Well, yes there is one major drawback...Growth. Your growth to be all you can be, to see your life through your eyes, not the eyes of anyone else. Friends and family may wonder at your new view of the world. They may admire or they may criticize. I suggest that, in either case, you smile—and move forward.

11

FOOD FOR THOUGHT

There were seven wonders in the ancient world: the Great Pyramids of Geiser, the Colossus of Rhodes, the Lighthouse of Alexandria, the Mausoleum at Halicarnassus, the Temple of Artemis, the statue of Zeus at Olympia, and the Hanging Gardens at Babylon.

Let me add one more wonder of the world that God tried to hide from us, so we would appreciate it when we found it. God thought hard and long where can I hide it? God said, "If I hide it in deepest part of the ocean, someday man will create a watercraft that will find it." God was thinking more and said, "If I hide it in deep space, someday man will create a rocket and will find it. Then God thought about, "I will hide it in place where man will never look, in-between his ears and I will call it his mind." That's what we have been talking about here using the Big Four Process to explore that amazing place between your ears.

Remember a journey of 1,000 miles starts with your first step. You have more power than you know, and by using the Big Four Process, you can start your journey by changing your dreams into your reality, no matter what it is.

As once said by Zig Ziglar, the first cassette series on positive thinking that I listened to in 1979, "See You at the Top."

Thank you for your time.

Dr. Anthony DeCanto

ACKNOWLEDGMENTS

First, my parents who taught me that, "You can be or do, whatever you choose." They never said to me, "You're not good enough." This was important to me due to the fact my father could not read or write. Leaving school in the third grade only left my father with an obvious lack of book knowledge, but what amazed me was his knowledge of LIFE.

Without my parent's support, I would not be able to thank all my patients for their trust and belief in me. Every one of my patients, past, present, and future, led me to authoring this book, *Four Steps to A Better Life*. I am eternally grateful for each patient that helped me change the world, because of what I learned from my experiences and with them.

ABOUT THE AUTHOR

Dr. Anthony DeCanto has been in the health care profession for over 43 years, and still going strong. Dr. DeCanto has degrees from Delaware Valley College in Pennsylvania, National College of Chiropractic in Illinois, and earned a Doctor of Medical and Health Humanities from Drew University in New Jersey.

Dr. DeCanto opened his Chiropractic office in 1979. Over the past 43 years, Dr. DeCanto has received Chiropractic awards, produced a cable show on health and wellbeing, recorded and marketed ten CDs on Chiropractic marketing and communication strategies, secured two patents for a neck and back brace, and taught workshops at adult education and at Somerset School of Massage. He has earned certification as a Reiki Master, Integrated Energy Therapy Master Instructor, a Certified Ordained Minister, and spent ten weeks in Sedona, Arizona and Mount Shasta, California studying metaphysical meditation.

Dr. Anthony DeCanto's major accomplishment will be to change the world by creating a new healing art through the knowledge in *Four Steps to A Better Life.* Dr. Anthony DeCanto points out, be careful what you ask for, because you may receive in a way that is unexpected, as described in this book.

Dr. DeCanto believes that an award does not make the person, the person makes the award. He is not a survivor because a survivor works from fear, not love. Every person has core beliefs and understanding that directs them and guides them through their journey in life. Dr. DeCanto knows that the highest vibration is love and with this information, everyone can become a winner.

CONTACT INFORMATION

YouTube Channel

Findyourblocks.com

Premier Research Vitamins

You can place an order or make an appointment by going to Findyourblocks.com. You can also email any questions to Questionforhealth@gmail.com

- To find out more about The Big Four Process, go to YouTube Channel first and then type *Dr Tony The Big Four Process.*
- When you sign up with Premier Research Vitamins, you will receive free valuable information to help balance the physical aspect of The Big Four Process.
- If you are in the healing art profession and would like to use The Big Four Process in your practice, contact the author for more information at Questionforhealth@gmail.com

Made in the USA
Middletown, DE
26 February 2023

25669033R00076